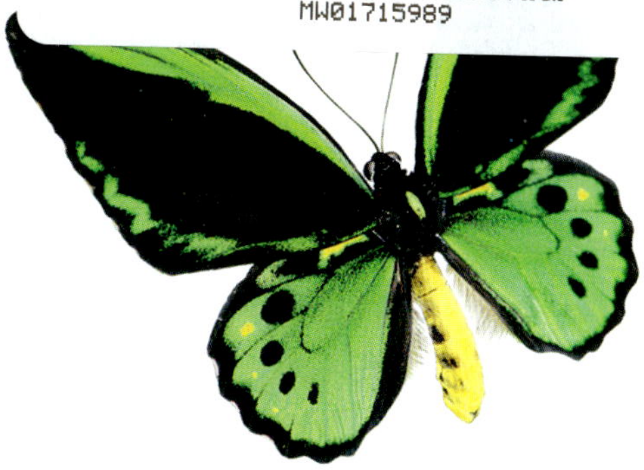

Australian WILDLIFE VERSES

Ric Nattrass

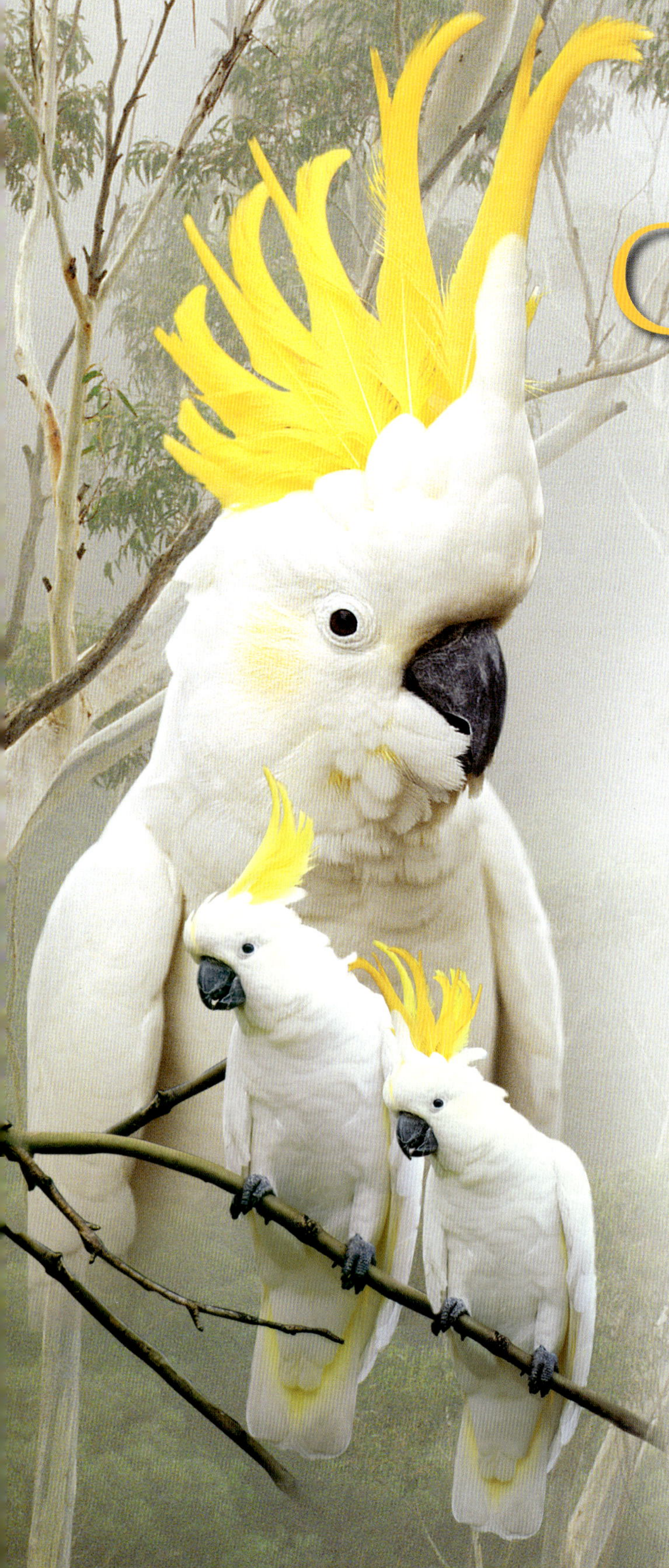

Cockatoo

Cocka-nought, cocka-one, cockatoo.
What a height, what a sight, what a view!
With a coat white as snow
Yellow crest he can throw
To his knees if he please
With a hiss and a sneeze!
Whoops, he's gone! Did you see where he flew?
Cocka-nought, cocka-one, cockatoo!

Cocka-nought, cocka-one, cockatoo.
What a cheek, what a beak, what a chew!
What a flock in a tree
If you look you can see
That there's always an eye
On the ground and the sky
And just why? Well, you'd laugh if you knew.
Cocka-nought, cocka-one, cockatoo!

About the Verse: Perhaps best known of Australia's thirteen species of crested parrots, the Sulphur-crested Cockatoo, *Cacatua galerita*, is also popular as a cage bird and family pet. Feeding in large flocks, their numbers ensure "that there's always an eye on the ground and the sky", making an unexpected attack by a predator very unlikely to succeed.

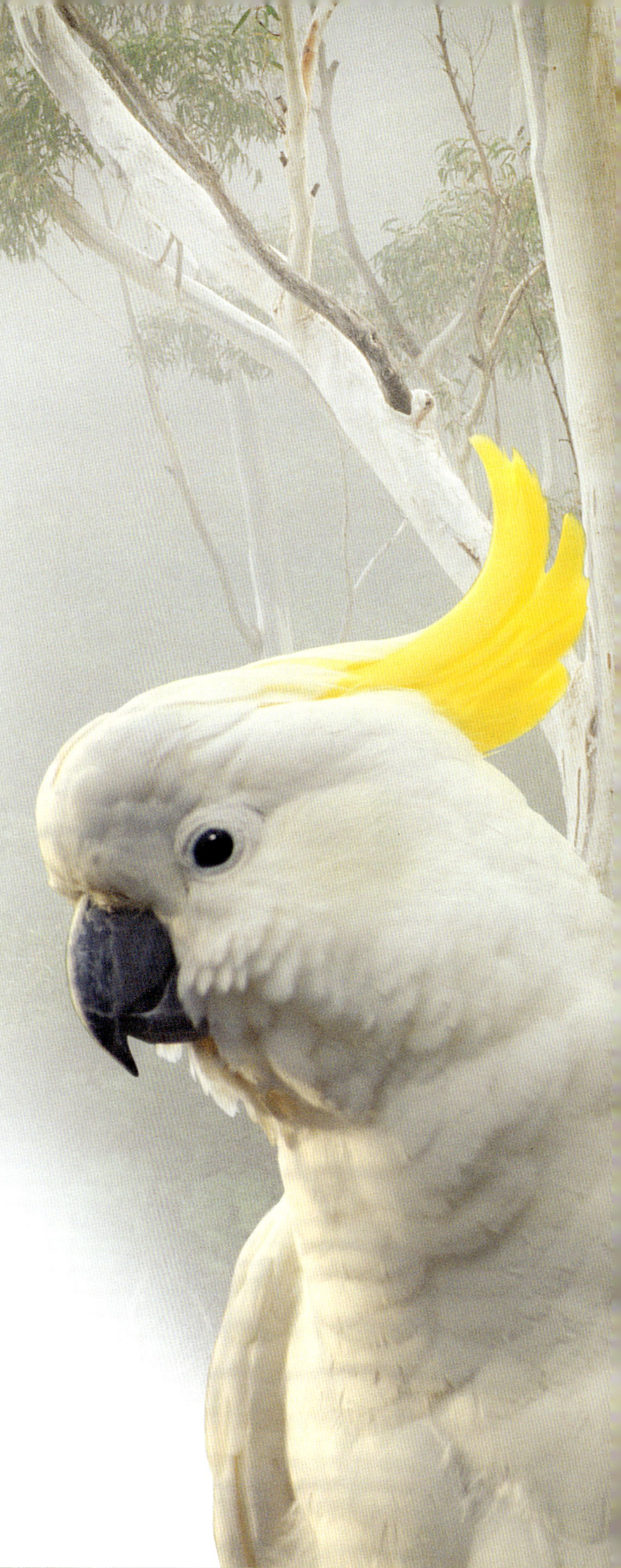

Cocka-nought, cocka-one, cockatoo.
What a peach of a screech, what a blue!
What a sight in the air
If you look way up there
You will see as he goes
How he tucks in his toes
Whoops, he's gone! Did you see where he flew?
Cocka-nought, cocka-one, cockatoo!

Cocka-nought, cocka-one, cockatoo.
What a sight, what a height, what a view!
What a coat white as snow
Yellow crest he can throw
To his knees if he please
With a scream and a sneeze!
Whoops, he's gone! Did you see where he flew?
Cocka-nought, cocka-one, cockatoo!

In Australian slang a "cockatoo" is a lookout, a person designated to keep watch and warn of approaching danger. During illegal gambling games the approaching danger was usually the local police officer. "And just why – well, you'd laugh if you knew".

Kakatua is a Malay word for large parrot-like birds.

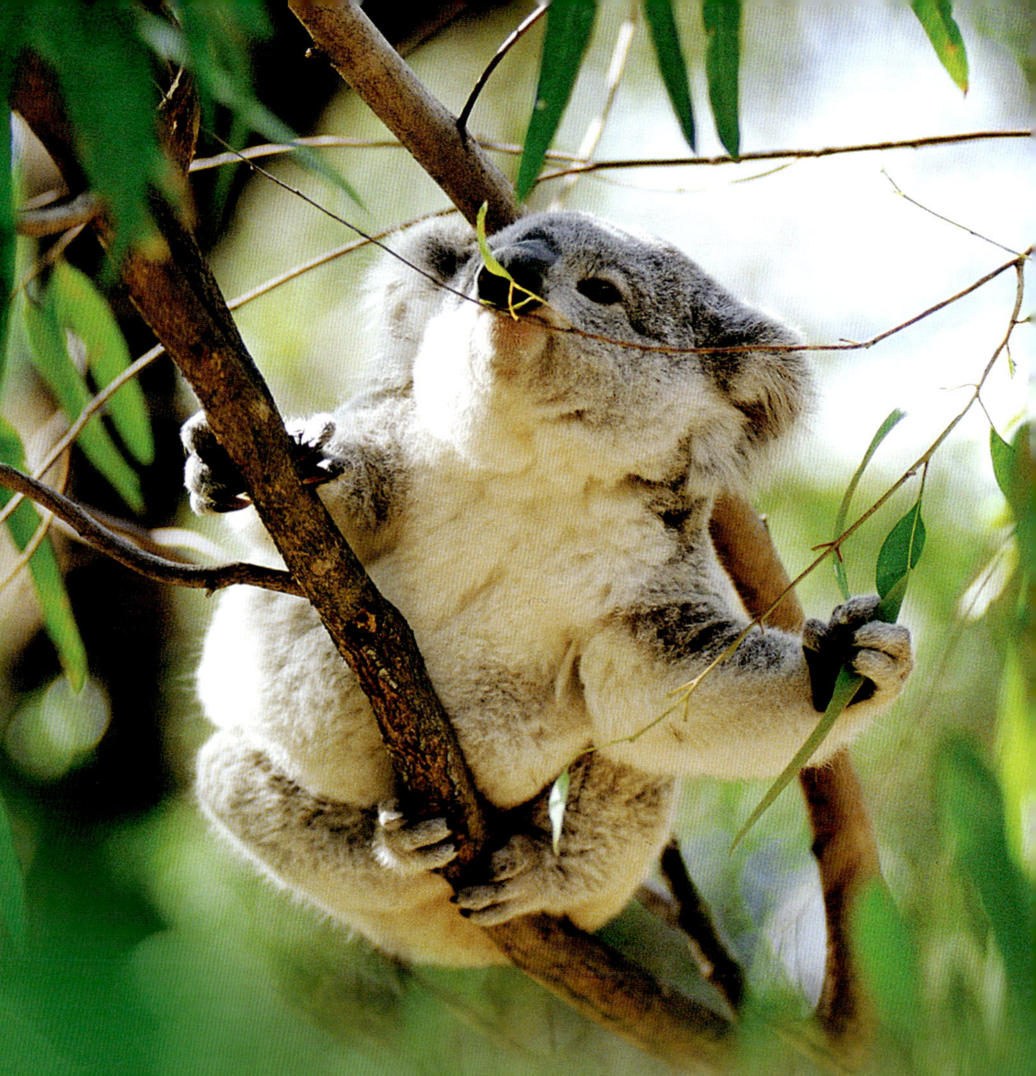

PLEASE CALL ME KOALA

I'm Australia's favourite son
And daughter — I'm the chosen one.
This is a heavy cross to bear —
So please call me Koala.

When I'm a baby, just a bub,
Please call me joey not a cub,
That's a word I'm loath to hear —
And please call me Koala.

My mum is pouched, and that's to start.
True bears and we are worlds apart,
And we're not ursine, I can swear —
So please call me Koala.

My world consists of forest trees
In which I sit and eat the leaves.
Please stop my world from going bare —
And please call me Koala!

About the Verse: It is surprising how often we hear the word "bear" attached to the Koala even though it is quite well known that the Koala is a marsupial, and not a bear. The use of the word "cub" rather than "joey" for the young koala that rides on its mother's back helps to keep the confusion alive.

True bears, are the ursines (*ursus* is Latin for bear): black and brown bears and polar bears. They are members of the Order Carnivore, which also includes wolves, cats, seals and other animal-eating mammals. There are no native bears in Australia.

The Koala's closest relative is the wombat.

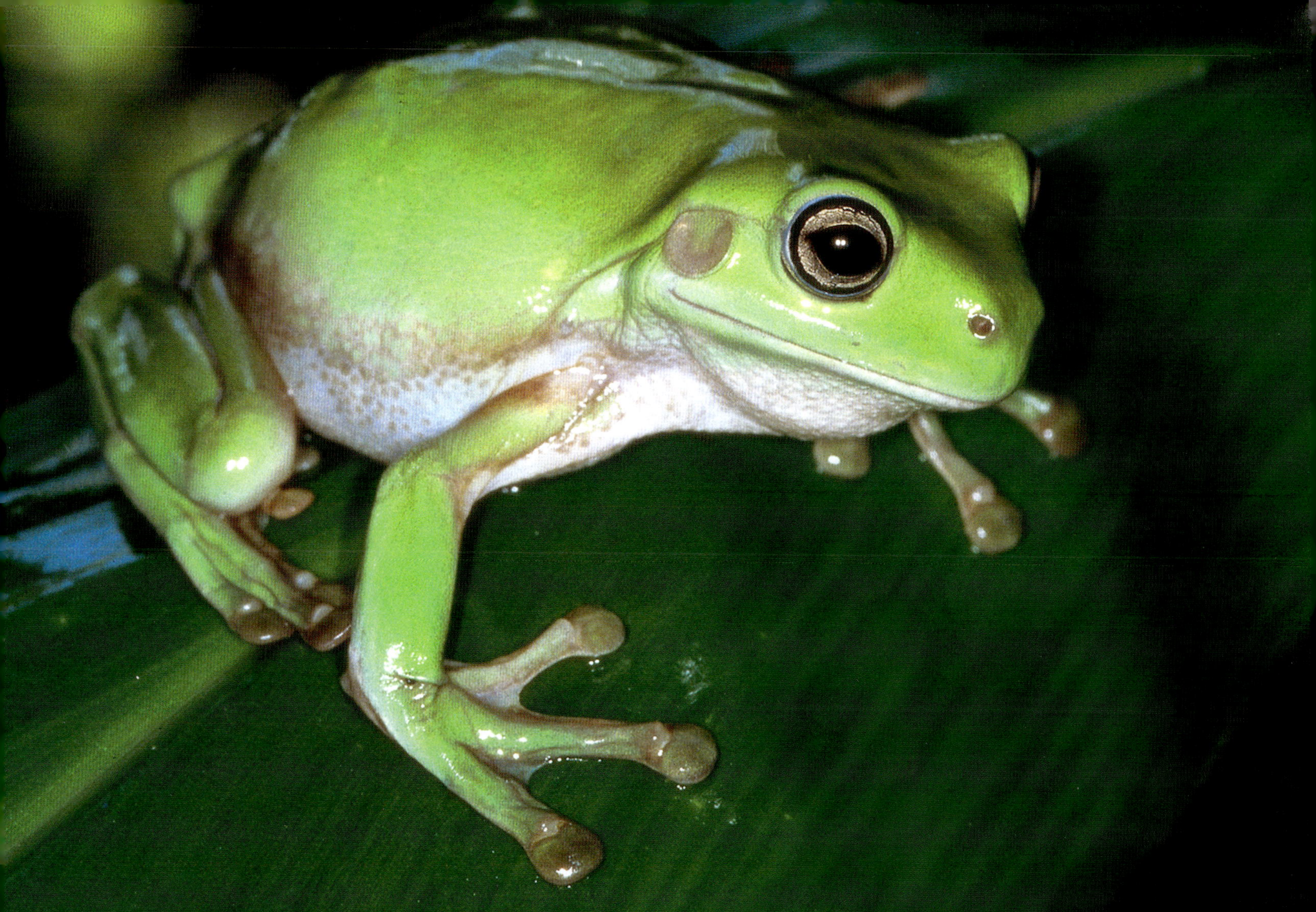

I'M A FROG

Don't stain it
Don't drain it
Don't spill it
Don't kill it
Don't fell it
And sell it
And fill it with folk.

It's a creek
It's a soak
It's a swamp
It's a bog
But it's vital to me
It's my home...
I'm a frog!

About the Verse: With the recent extinction of six species of native Australian frogs, the future of all remaining species is uncertain.

The disastrous extinctions happened when a microfungus, *Batrachochytrium dendrobatidis*, was accidentally introduced into frog environments.

Frog breeding and living spaces need to be carefully considered before being destroyed to construct buildings, roads and dams.

Many of the presently threatened frogs are tiny and known only to experts and keen froggers, but they are nonetheless precious for all their diminutive size.

MAGIC MAGPIE

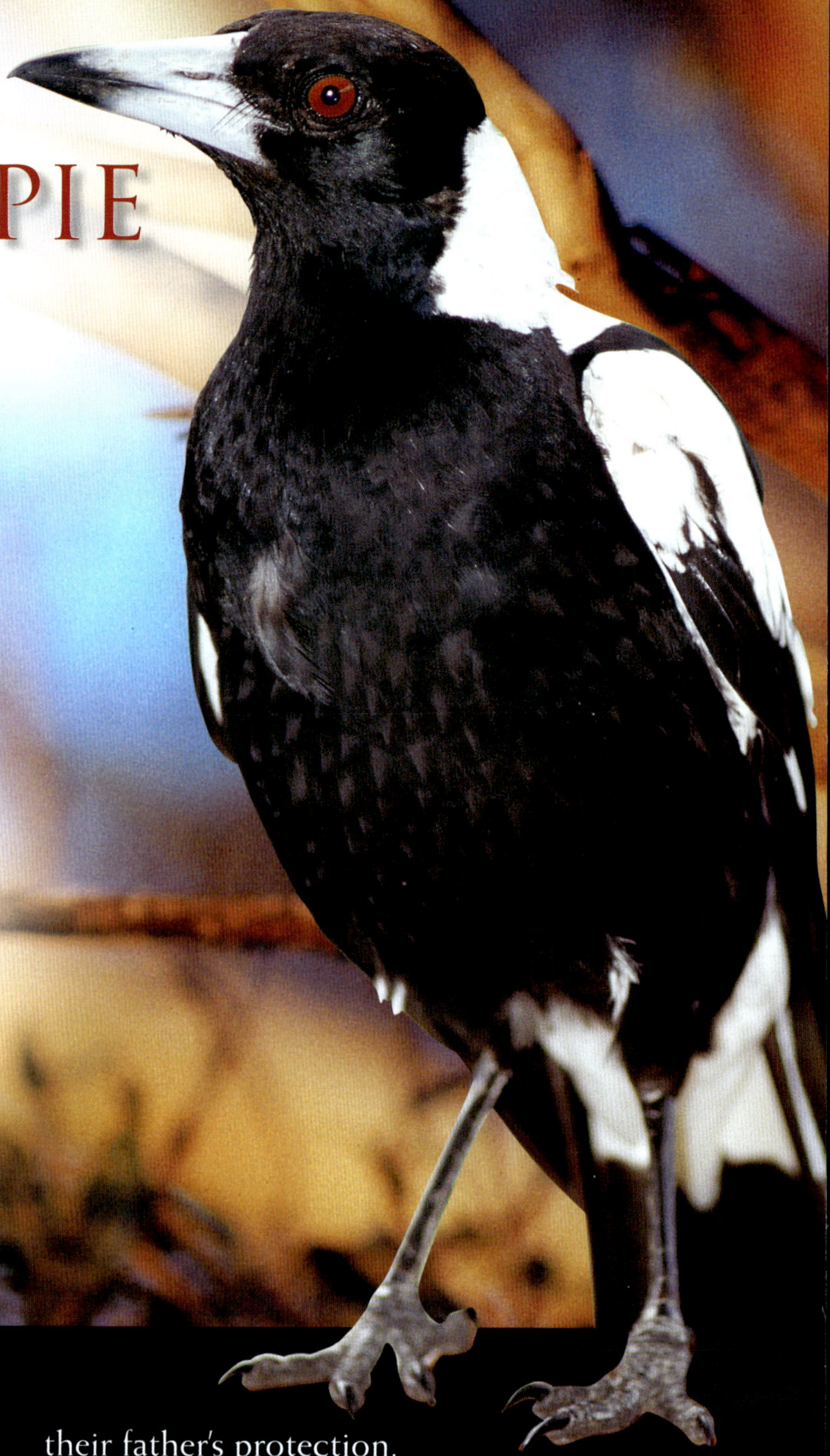

So brilliant black
And snowy white,
On powered wings
To dizzy height,
And soaring up
Till out of sight —
So flies the Magic Magpie.

His mate and babies
Are his might.
To keep them safe
For them he'll fight,
And lead the chorus
At first light —
So sings the Magic Magpie.

About the Verse: The Australian Magpie, *Gymnorhina tibicen*, is not related to the European magpies from which it gets its common name but resembles them in its black and white plumage.

The Australian bird has a reputation for vigorously defending its territory, nest, mate and young against humans but only when provoked, either deliberately or accidentally.

The most common cause of provocation by humans in the urban environment is when flightless chicks, dislodged from the nest, are rescued by caring people and removed from their father's protection.

He simply does not understand what's happening. From that time on he sees humans as predators and will attempt to drive them out of the breeding territory each nesting season.

This behaviour has made the Magpie the single most popular native animal to be used as a club emblem in all three codes of football.

By contrast, *tibicen* in Latin means "flute player", reflecting the other, more endearing characteristic of this well known bird of back yards, golf courses, parks and schoolgrounds.

KANGAROO

My arms are small,
My legs are tall,
My coat is warm
Against the storm,
And I can flail
A great thick tail;
For I'm a kangaroo.

My big round eyes
Are brown and wise,
Designed for sight
In blackest night,
I've radar ears
Like tips of spears;
For I'm a kangaroo.

And I can bound
Across the ground
At super speed
When I've a need.
There's no "enough",
I'll never puff;
For I'm a kangaroo!

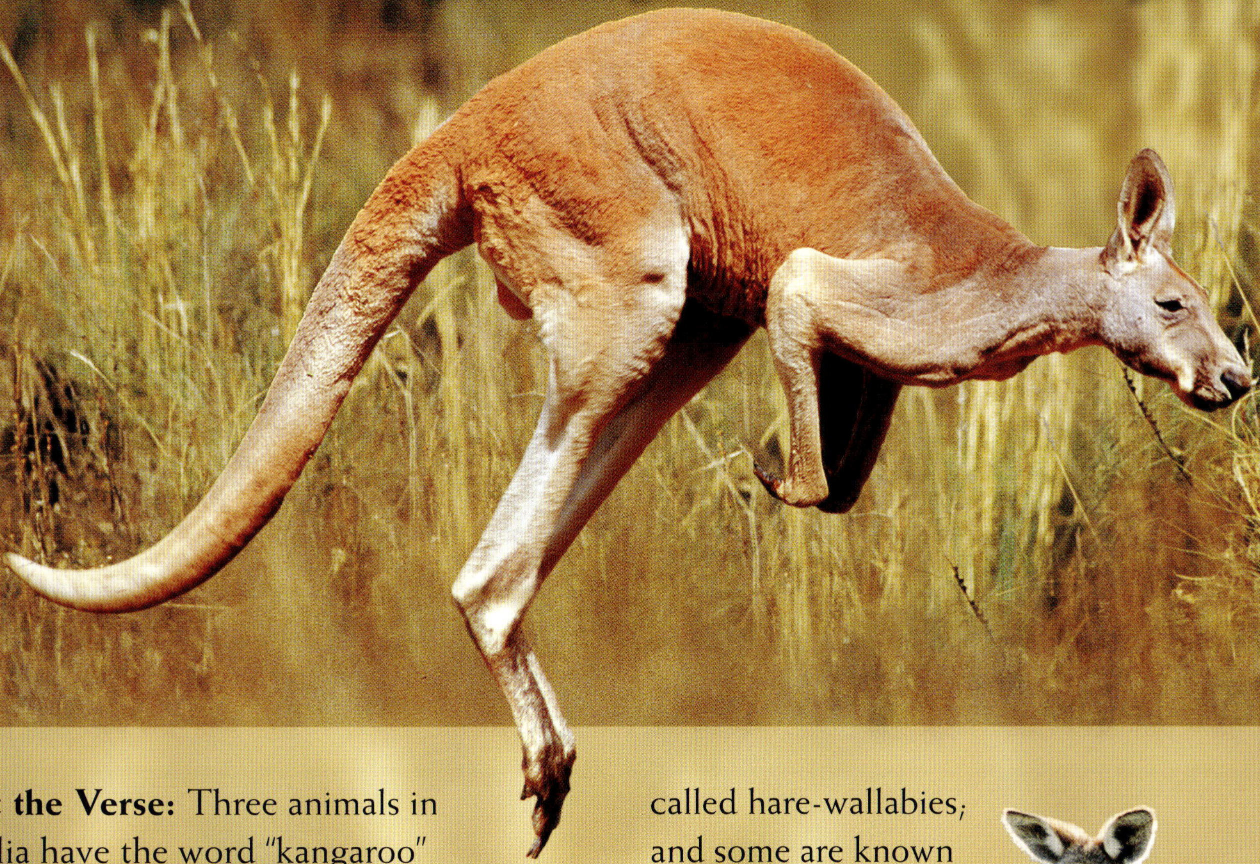

About the Verse: Three animals in Australia have the word "kangaroo" as part of their common name. They are the Eastern Grey Kangaroo, *Macropus giganteus*, the Western Grey Kangaroo, *Macropus fuliginosis*, and the Red Kangaroo, *Macropus rufus*. "Kangaroo" is a close approximation of the word in a northern Queensland Aboriginal language.

However, there are about sixty species in the group of animals we call kangaroos: three are known as wallaroos; the majority are known as wallabies; very small kangaroo cousins are called hare-wallabies; and some are known by other indigenous words such as "bettong" and "quokka".

As well as appearing on the Australian coat of arms opposite the Emu, the classic, unmistakable shape of the kangaroo is known to all the world as the white silhouette on the bright red tail of every Qantas aircraft.

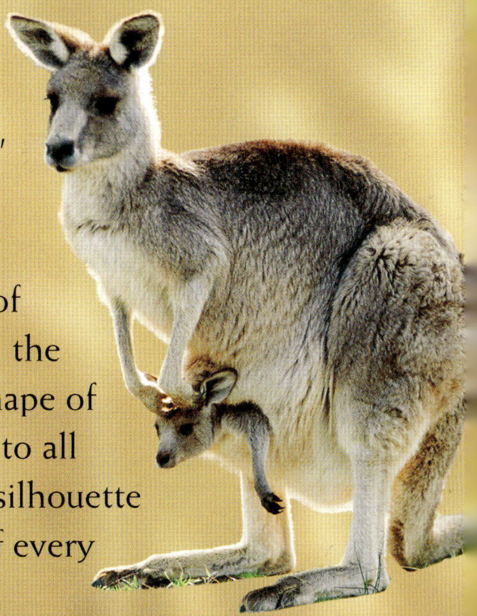

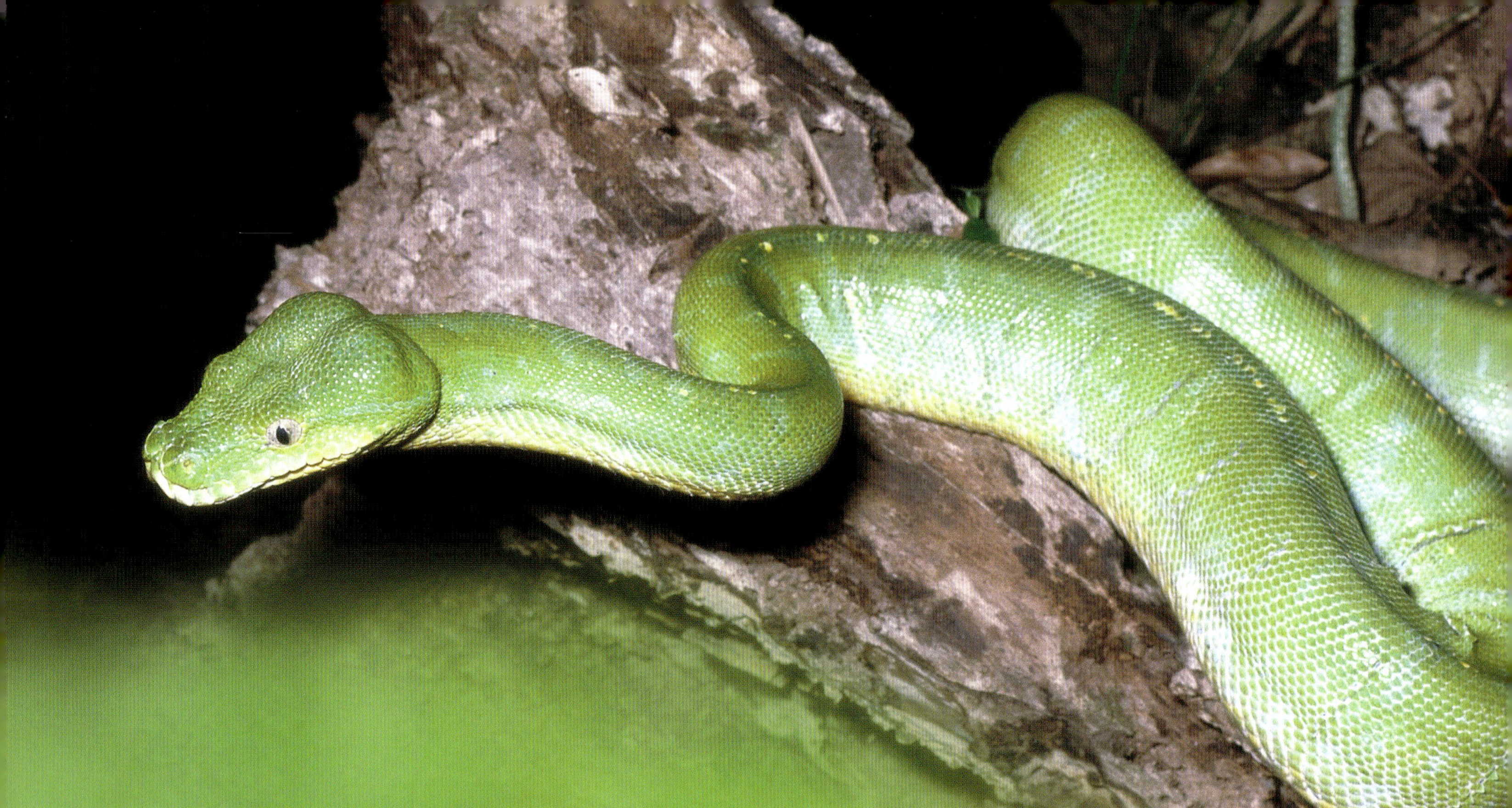

SNAKES

We're all a bit weird about snakes,
The sight of one give us the shakes.
But isn't it sad
If we treat all as bad
And chase them with shovels and rakes?

Snake myths abound, don't contrive one.
Of its life we must never deprive one.
For I'm sure that you knew
This one fact which is true:
That the only good snake is a live one!

About the Verse: A sudden and unexpected encounter with a snake will startle even the most experienced naturalist. While it is normal and healthy to be startled at the sudden sight of a snake and to flee what might be dangerous, it is not healthy to go after it with a stick. Ninety percent of all potentially fatal snakebites occur as a result of the "victim" trying to catch or kill one.

Where they occur naturally, snakes are also a vital part of the ecosystem. Many of the larger species feed at least to some extent on rodents. Rodent plagues still occur from time to time and are very expensive to treat. Why harm the local rat catcher?

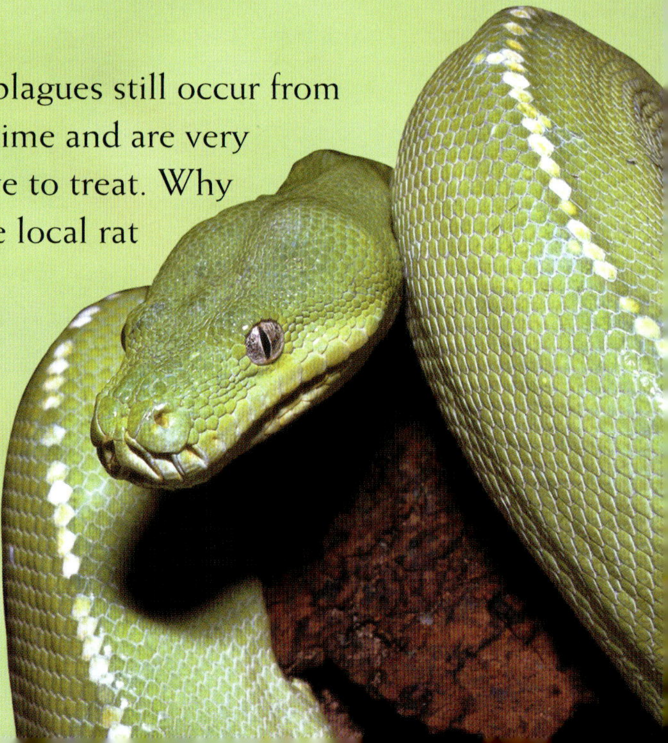

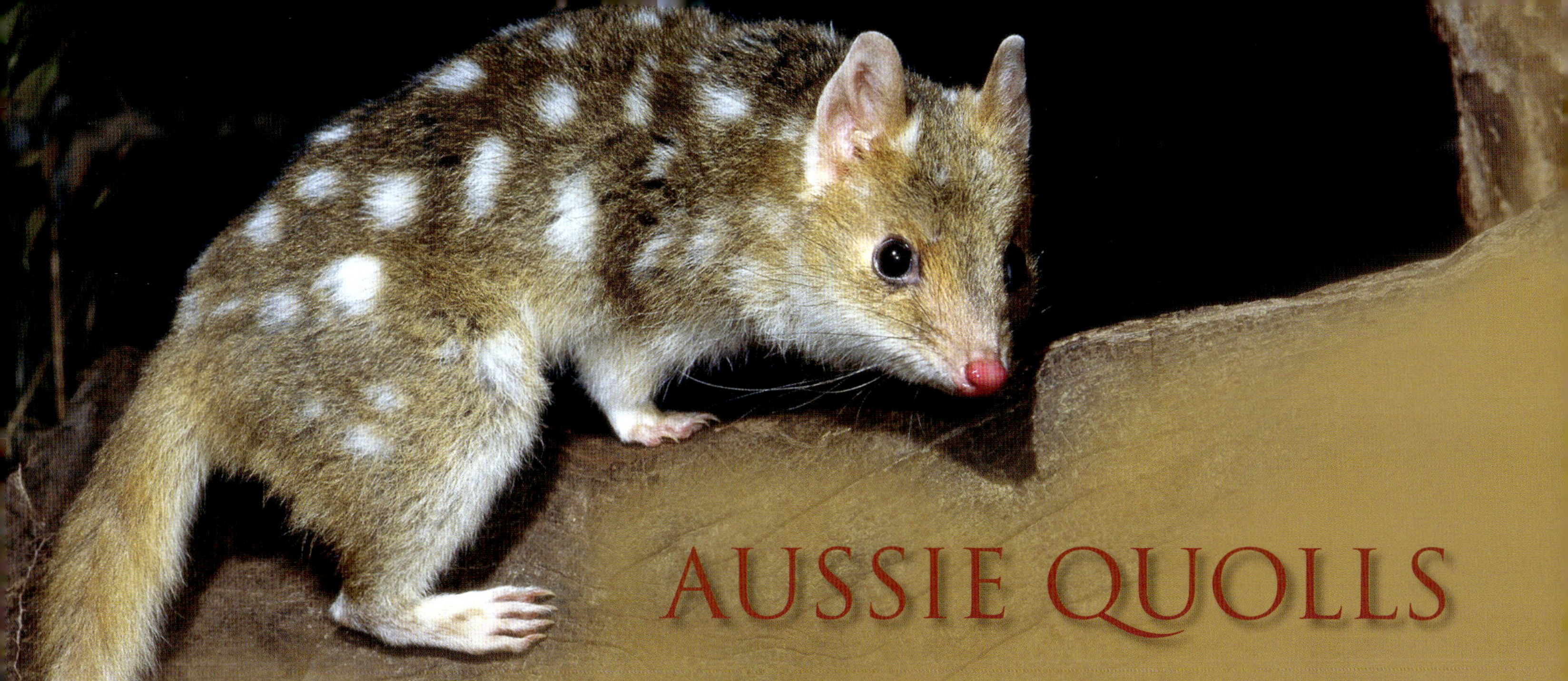

AUSSIE QUOLLS

Aussie quolls are most attractive,
Most are rare and only active
Where their forest homes are still intact.

Aussie quolls should not be messed with
For their gaping jaws are blessed with
Hugely glistening, razor-sharpened teeth.

Aussie quolls were once abundant;
I'm afraid they'll be redundant
On a list of dasyurid folk.

Aussie quolls are special to me.
Why they've gone is largely through me
Thinking that the world is just for us.

Aussie quolls are most attractive,
They will stay alive and active
If their forest homes remain intact.

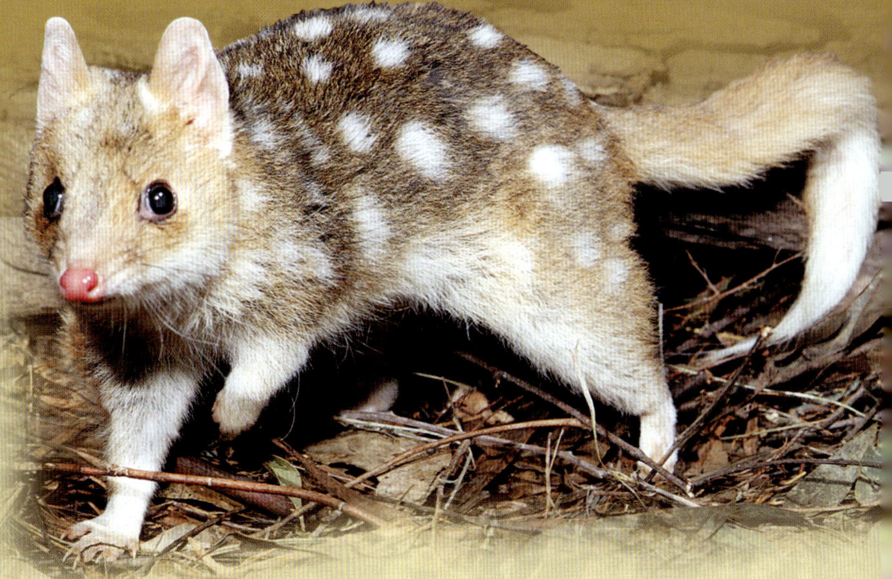

About the Verse: The carnivorous marsupials have proven to be among the most sensitive to European Australia. The largest and arguably most spectacular was the Tasmanian Tiger last seen alive on 6 September 1936 in the Hobart Zoo.

Its smaller relatives, the four species of Quolls, are all threatened wherever extensive changes are occurring to their forest habitats.

Once known as native cats, they were a well known feature of the Australian bush, even around the outer suburbs of the capital cities.

Sadly, this is no longer the case and, in fact, few people are even aware that these extraordinary marsupials actually exist.

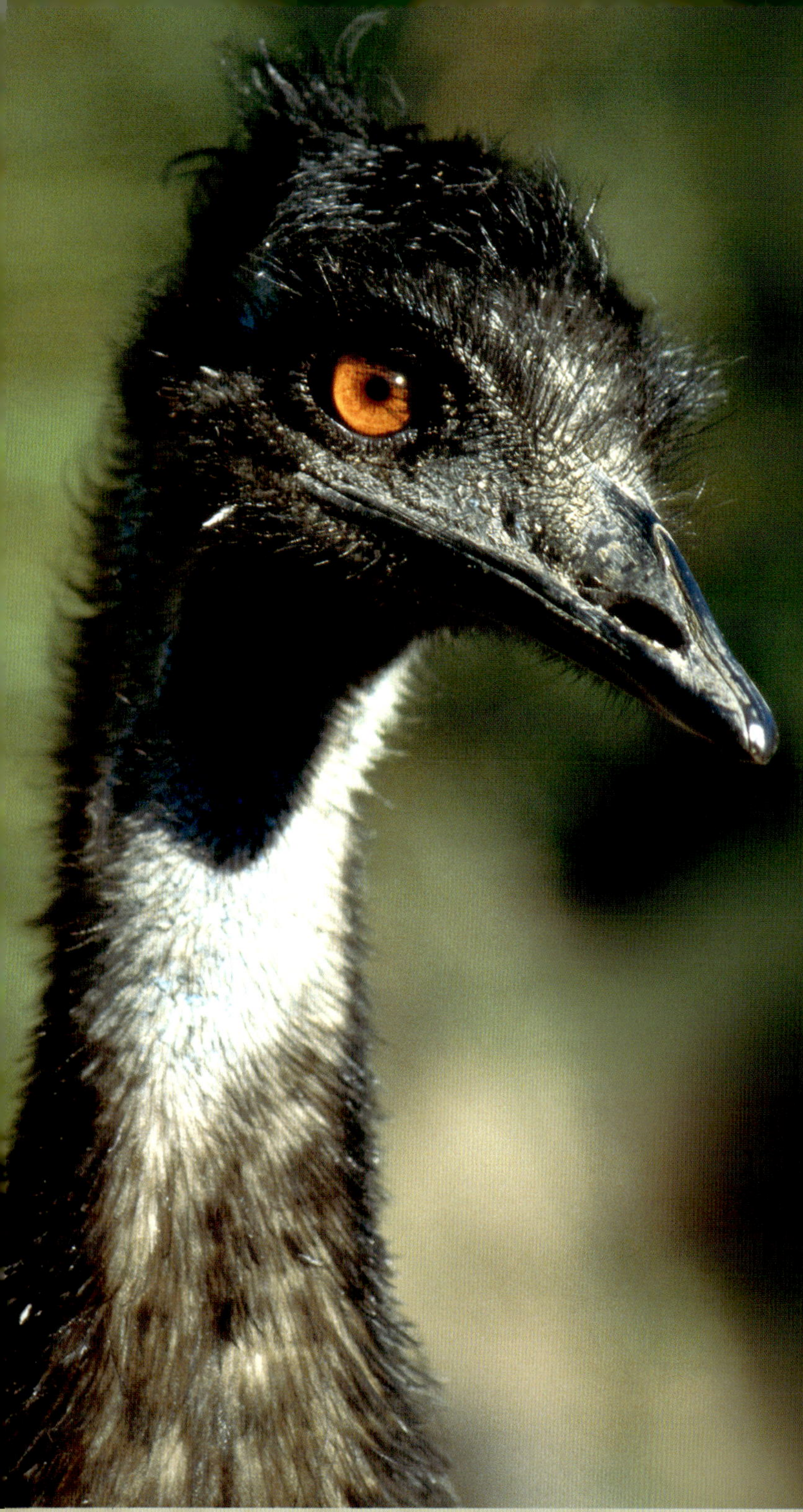

EMU

If you see a bird as large as me
With legs as round as a sapling tree
And feathers drooping to my knees,
Then… you've just seen an Emu.

If you hear a bird that booms not sings,
And sprints to flee because its wings
Are small and won't do flying things,
Then… you've just seen an Emu.

If you are a bird as huge as I
That never hoped to soar the sky
Nor envy ones who have to fly,
Then… you must be an Emu!

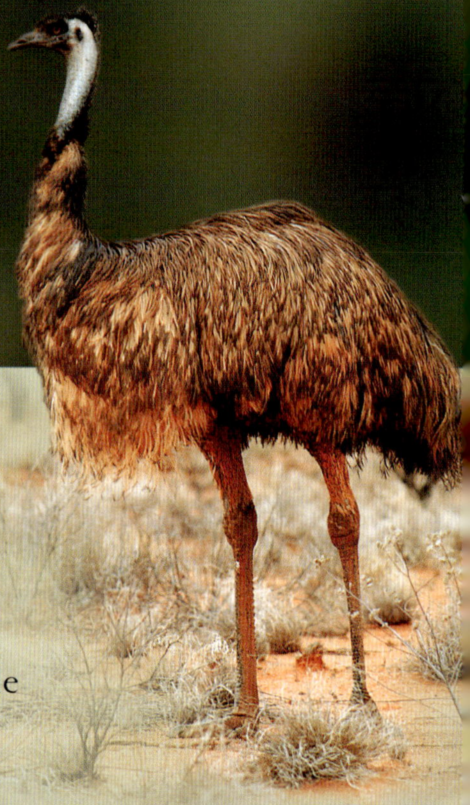

About the Verse: The taller, but lighter, of Australia's two giant ratite (flightless, having a flat breastbone) birds is the Emu.

Emus have a rather different approach to family life from most bird species. After mating with the male, the female deposits her twelve or so eggs directly on the ground and then leaves the male to care for them alone.

Dedicated to the task ahead, he sits continuously for eight weeks until the babies hatch, neither eating nor drinking during this all-important phase.

After the hatching, he continues as a single parent, nurturing and defending the chicks until their independence at about 18 months.

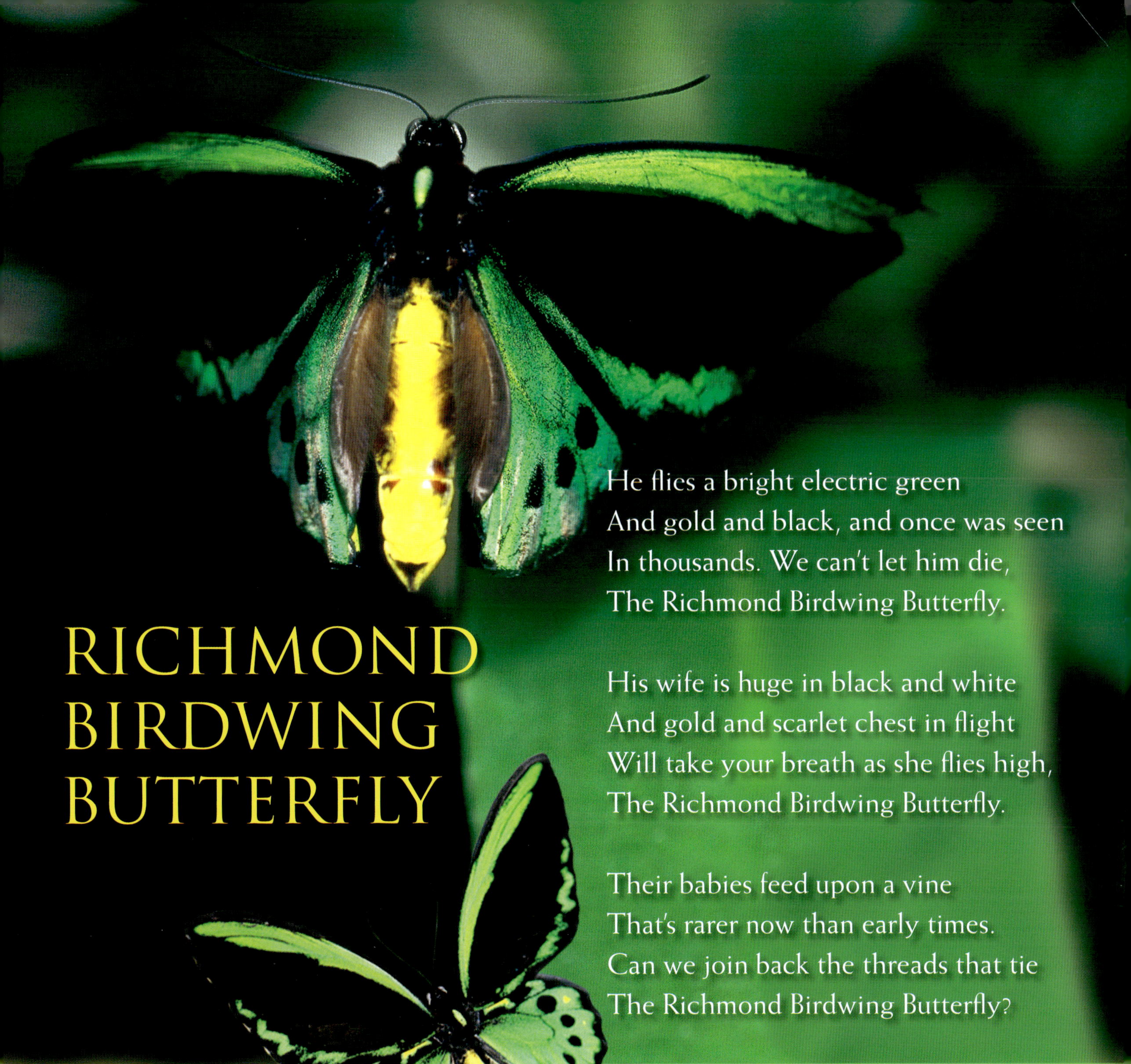

RICHMOND BIRDWING BUTTERFLY

He flies a bright electric green
And gold and black, and once was seen
In thousands. We can't let him die,
The Richmond Birdwing Butterfly.

His wife is huge in black and white
And gold and scarlet chest in flight
Will take your breath as she flies high,
The Richmond Birdwing Butterfly.

Their babies feed upon a vine
That's rarer now than early times.
Can we join back the threads that tie
The Richmond Birdwing Butterfly?

About the Verse:
The Richmond Birdwing Butterfly gets its common name from the Richmond River in New South Wales and its bird-sized wings. It is found on the coast of northern New South Wales and southern Queensland to about Gympie.

It is an endangered species, mainly due to the loss of the rainforest in which birdwing vines grow and on which its caterpillars feed.

An introduced South American vine, Dutchman's Pipe Vine, is closely related to the Australian vines. Female butterflies are strongly attracted and lay their eggs on it, but the caterpillars die when they feed on it.

A birdwing butterfly recovery program encourages people to plant the native vine wherever they can and to avoid the deadly exotic vine. There is evidence that this program is having a positive effect.

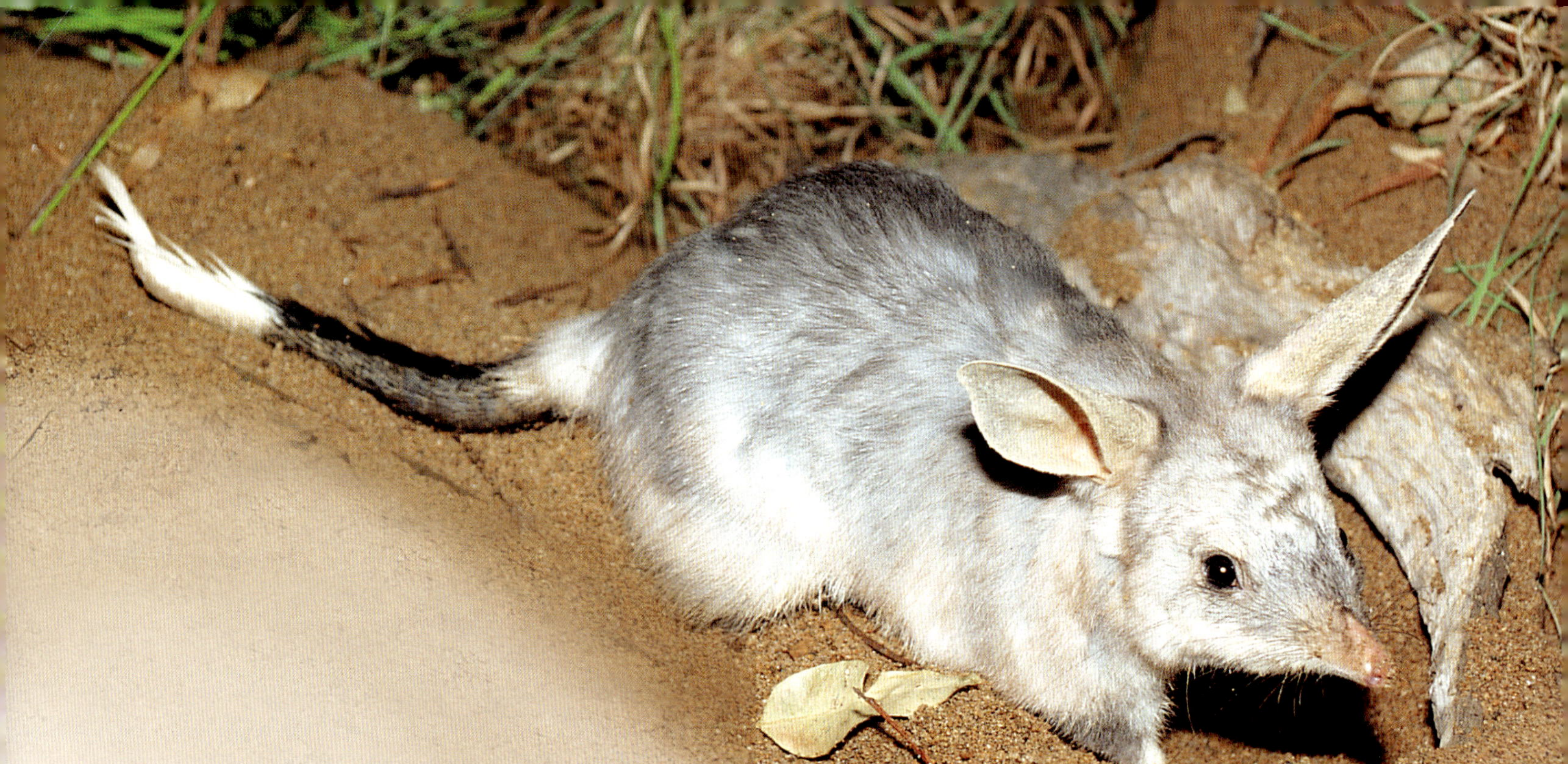

BILBY

There no hill be
Where the Bilby
Lives — it's dry and flat.

Once, in thousands,
In came cows and
Rabbit, sheep and fox and cat.

There's a worry
Where they scurry
That there will be, soon, no Bilby.

Just imagine that!

About the Verse: The last living Lesser Bilby, *Macrotis leucura*, was reported in 1931 and this smaller of the two bilby species is now regarded as extinct. Although still living in the wild, by the 1970s the Greater Bilby, *Macrotis lagotis*, had been reduced to a few hundred and is considered a seriously endangered marsupial.

The Bilby is now the subject of a vigorous recovery program throughout Australia. The Save the Bilby Fund has provided a predator-proof fence at Currawinya National Park in central southern Queensland. Large numbers of captive-bred Bilbies have been released into the predator-proof enclosure, in the hope that they will thrive and eventually be released into the surrounding national park where they were once very common.

The word "bil-bi" is recorded from Wiradjuri, the language of the traditional owners of the central to southern New South Wales area. Other indigenous names include Dalgyte, Ninu, Marrura and Walpatjurri.

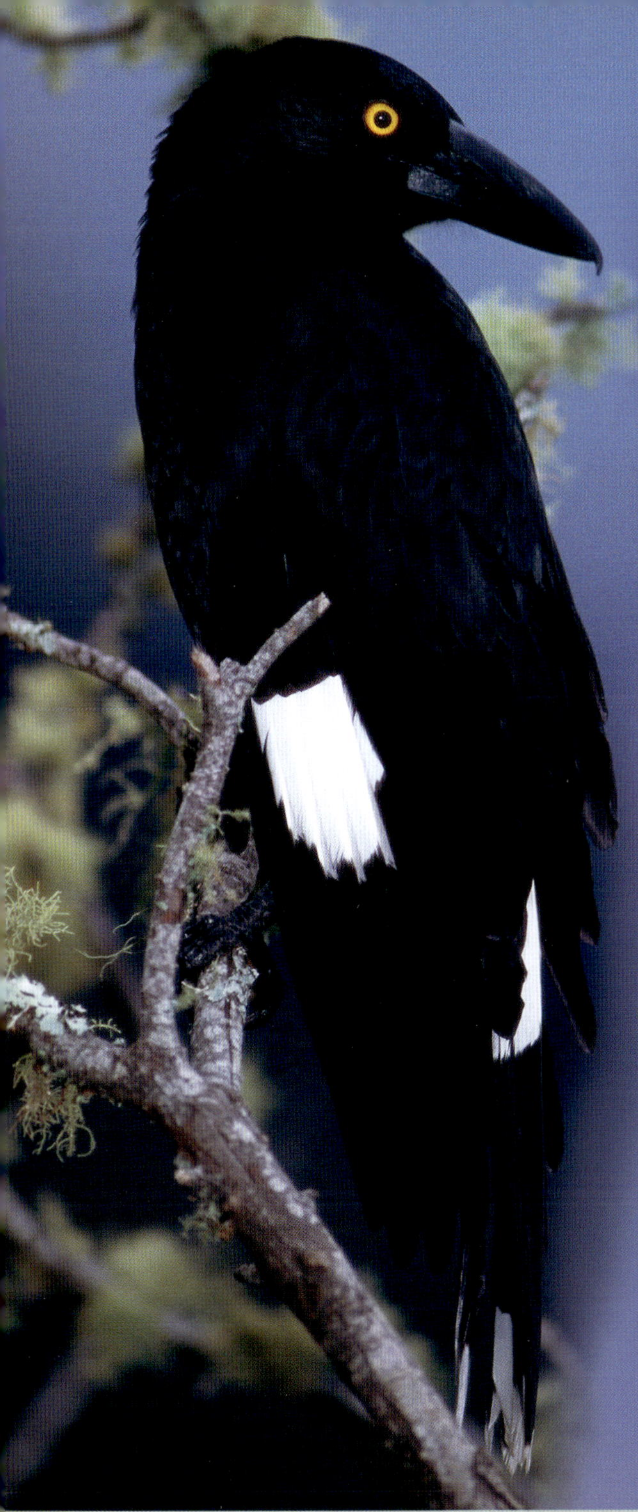

CURRAWONG

Oh Currawong, oh what a song,
The chirrahs fill the air
With sweet-a-wee, and I can see
Your brilliant yellow stare.

The seasons bring you to and fro,
Just why you come and where you go
Are secrets kept from me.

Oh Currawong, oh what a song,
The chirrahs fill the air,
On days wintry, where would I be
Bird, if you were not there?

The seasons bring you to and fro,
Just why you come and where you go
Are secrets kept from me.

About the Verse: In many parts of the Pied Currawong's range the birds are altitudinal migrants, moving to the lowlands during the colder months and returning to the highlands in summer.

Where they do this, their distinctive winter call of a chirrah followed by a looping whistle that rises then falls in an unbroken musical gliss, heralds winter.

Two other species are found in Australia: the Grey and the Black Currawongs.

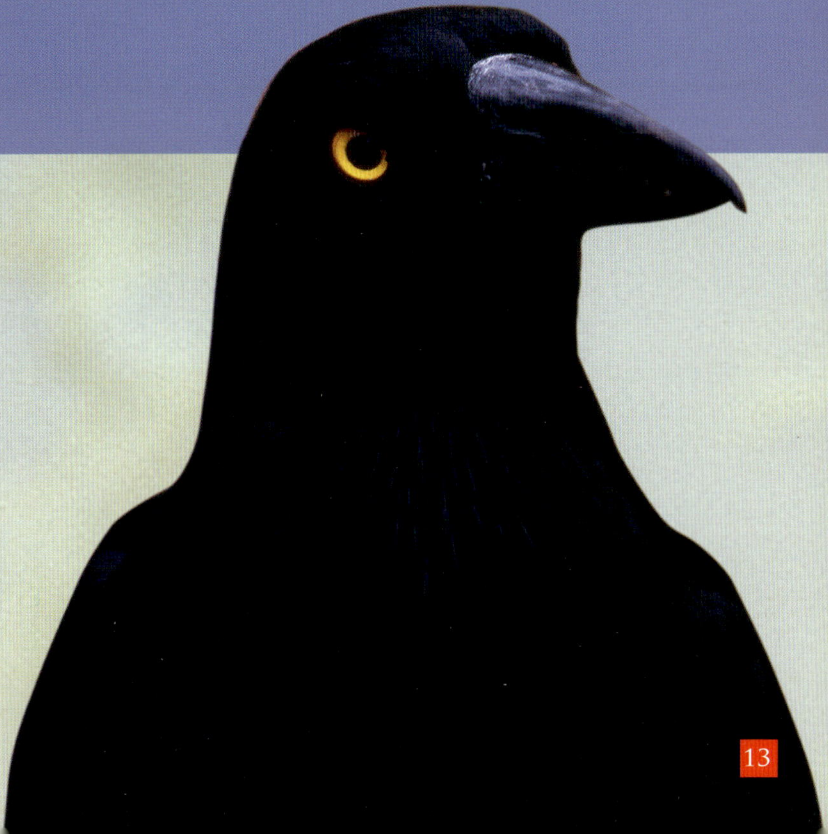

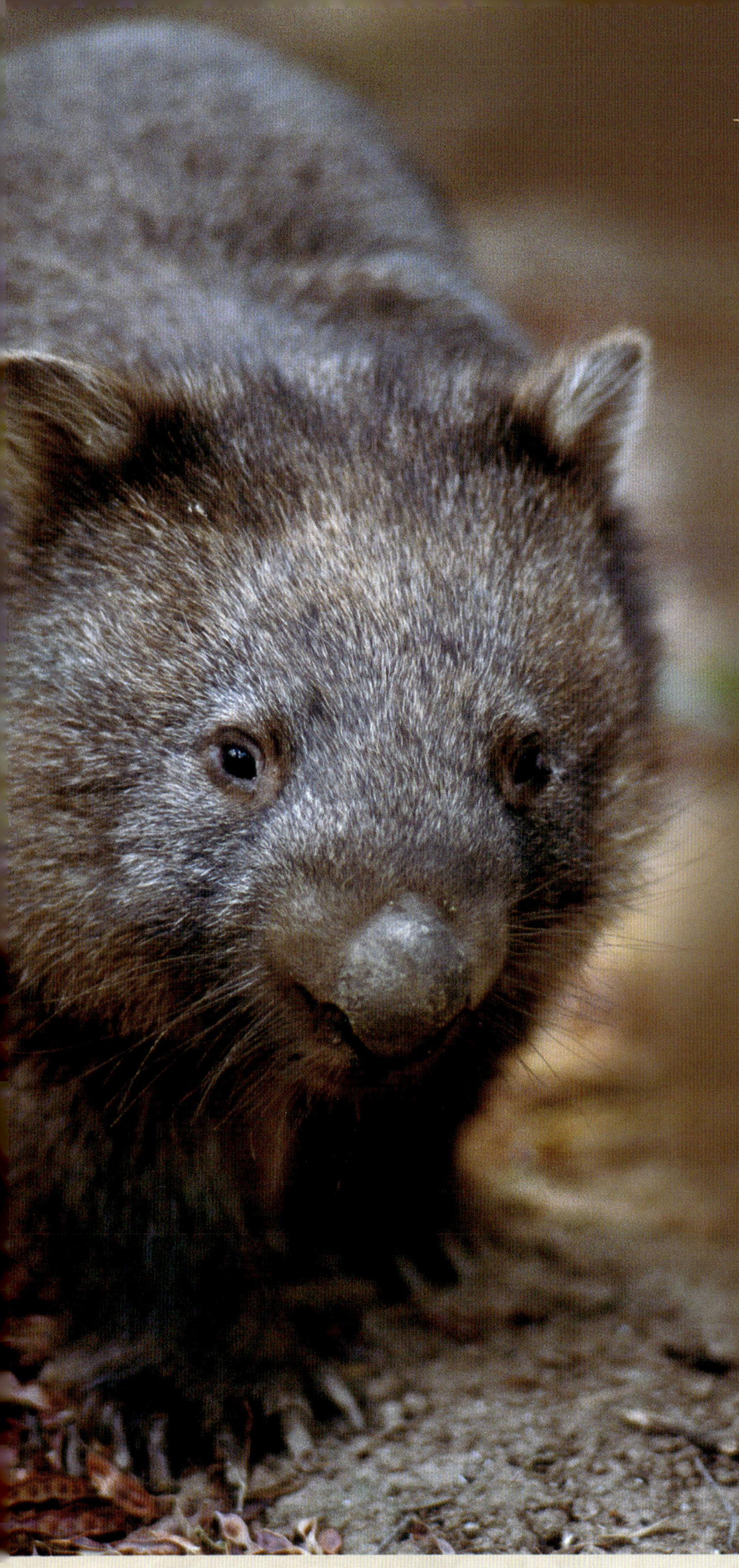

WOMBAT

There are furrows to the burrows
Where the furrowed burrow ends,
And the burrows that have furrows
Are where wombats have their dens.

And everybody really loves a wombat.

They are likely to be nightly,
Sometimes sprightly, seen by day.
Should their weight be judged unsightly?
By how much we cannot say.

But everybody really loves a wombat.

About the Verse: Of Australia's three species of wombats, the Common Wombat, *Vombatus ursinus*, is the most familiar. It is found from the south-eastern Queensland highlands to eastern South Australia and throughout Tasmania.

The Southern Hairy-nosed Wombat, *Lasiorhinus latifrons*, is restricted to the semi-arid regions where humans populations are low. It is common in its range, but its range is not very big, so it is not found in large numbers.

Densely furred in brown, I've heard;
The nose is quite outstanding.
Rumble-bedded, muddle-headed
Myths and fibs abounding.

And everybody really loves a wombat.

There are furrows to the burrows
Where the furrowed burrow ends,
And the burrows that have furrows
Are where wombats have their dens.

But everybody really loves a wombat.

Don't you?

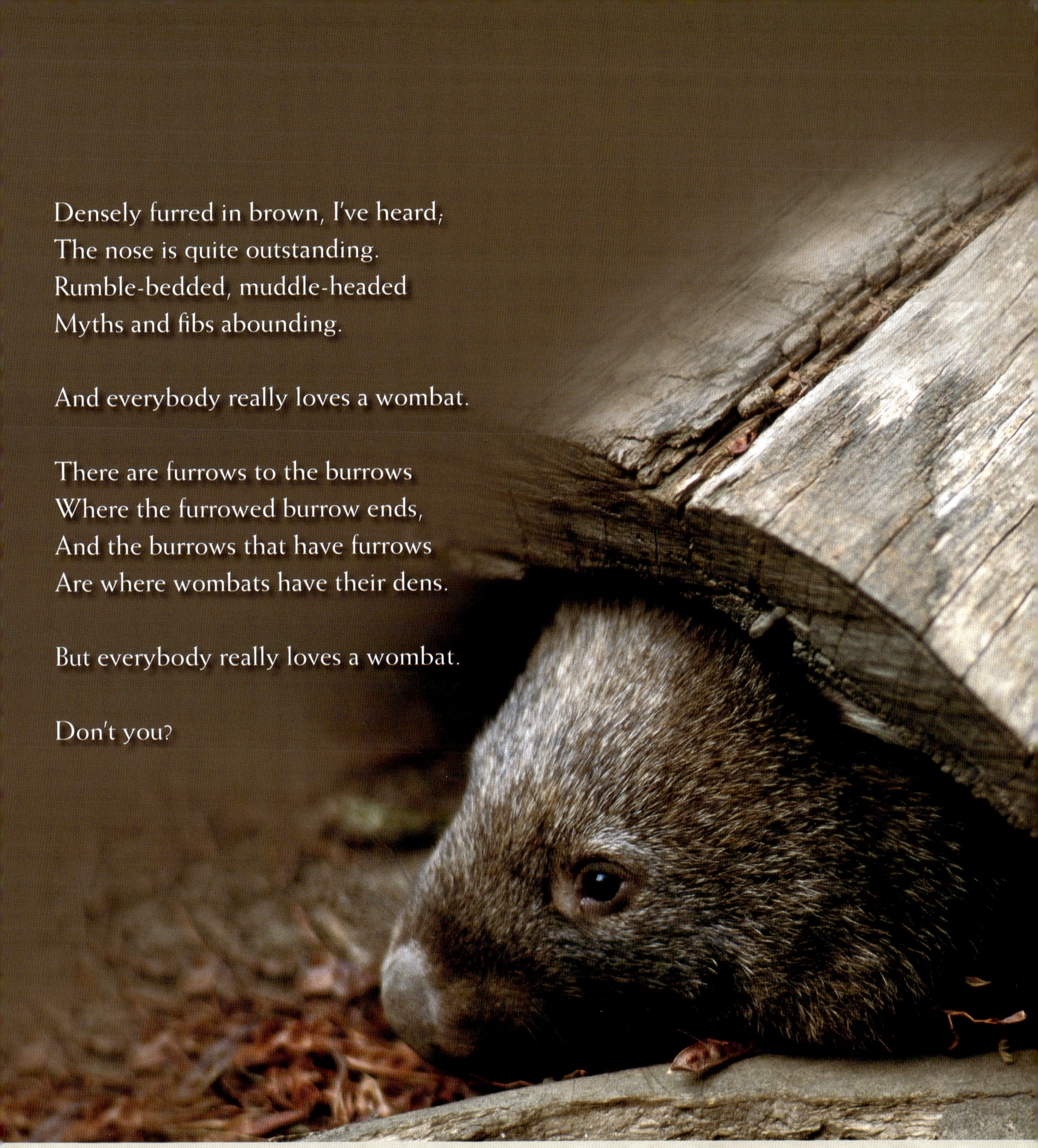

The Northern Hairy-nosed Wombat, *Lasiorhinus krefftii*, is Australia's most critically endangered large mammal. There are perhaps fewer than 100 individuals remaining near Clermont in central Queensland.

The wombat has been popularised in children's' literature as having a charming and endearing personality with a "muddled head". In fact, there is nothing muddle-headed about a wombat at all.

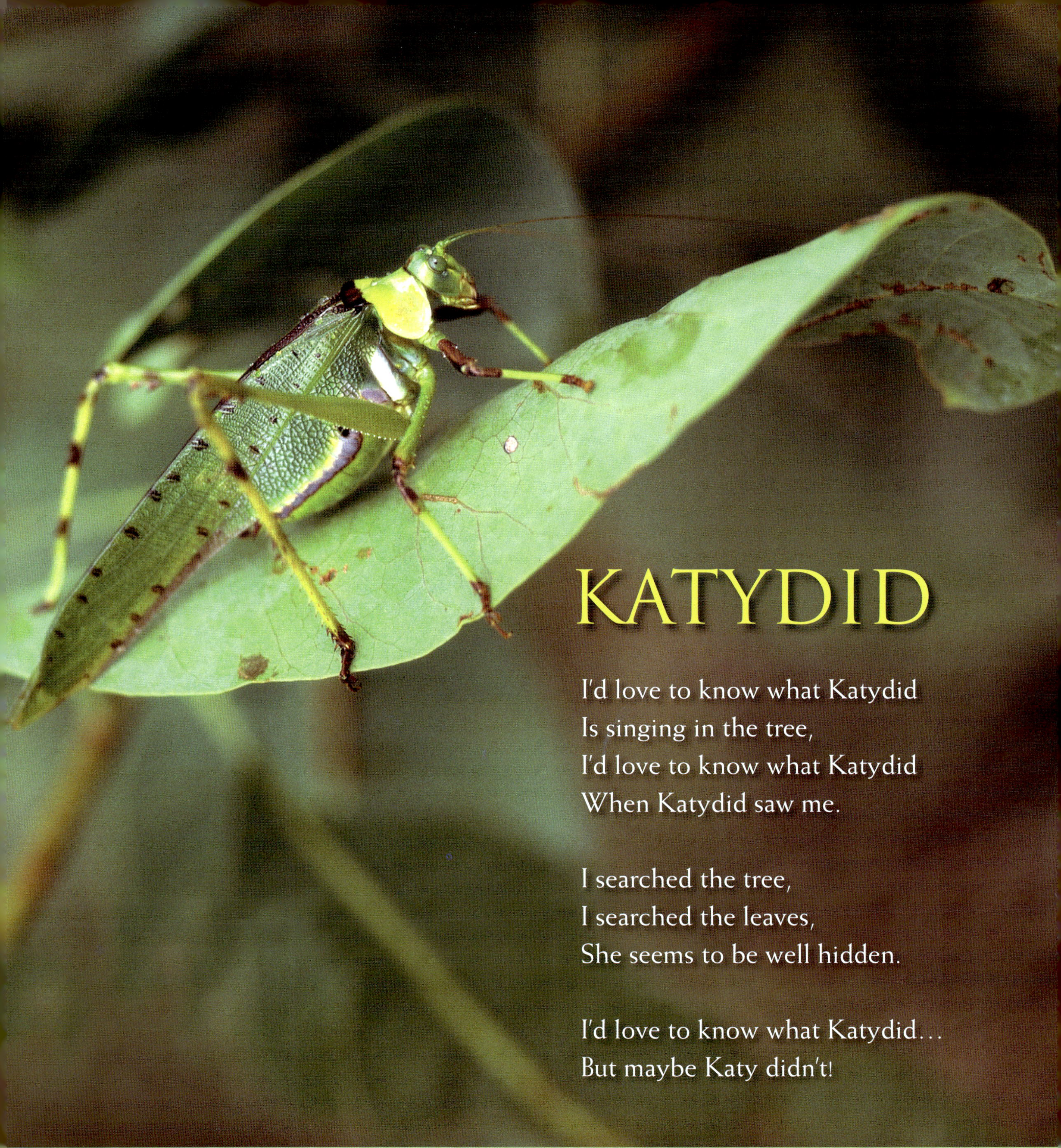

KATYDID

I'd love to know what Katydid
Is singing in the tree,
I'd love to know what Katydid
When Katydid saw me.

I searched the tree,
I searched the leaves,
She seems to be well hidden.

I'd love to know what Katydid…
But maybe Katy didn't!

About the Verse: They are insects of the Order Orthoptera, also called Long-horned Grasshoppers. They have strong back legs for jumping, and are related to grasshoppers, locusts and crickets.

They produce an audible call by rubbing wing edges on legs. In some species the result is a three note click which could be said to sound like "katy-did".
Katydids are found all over the world.

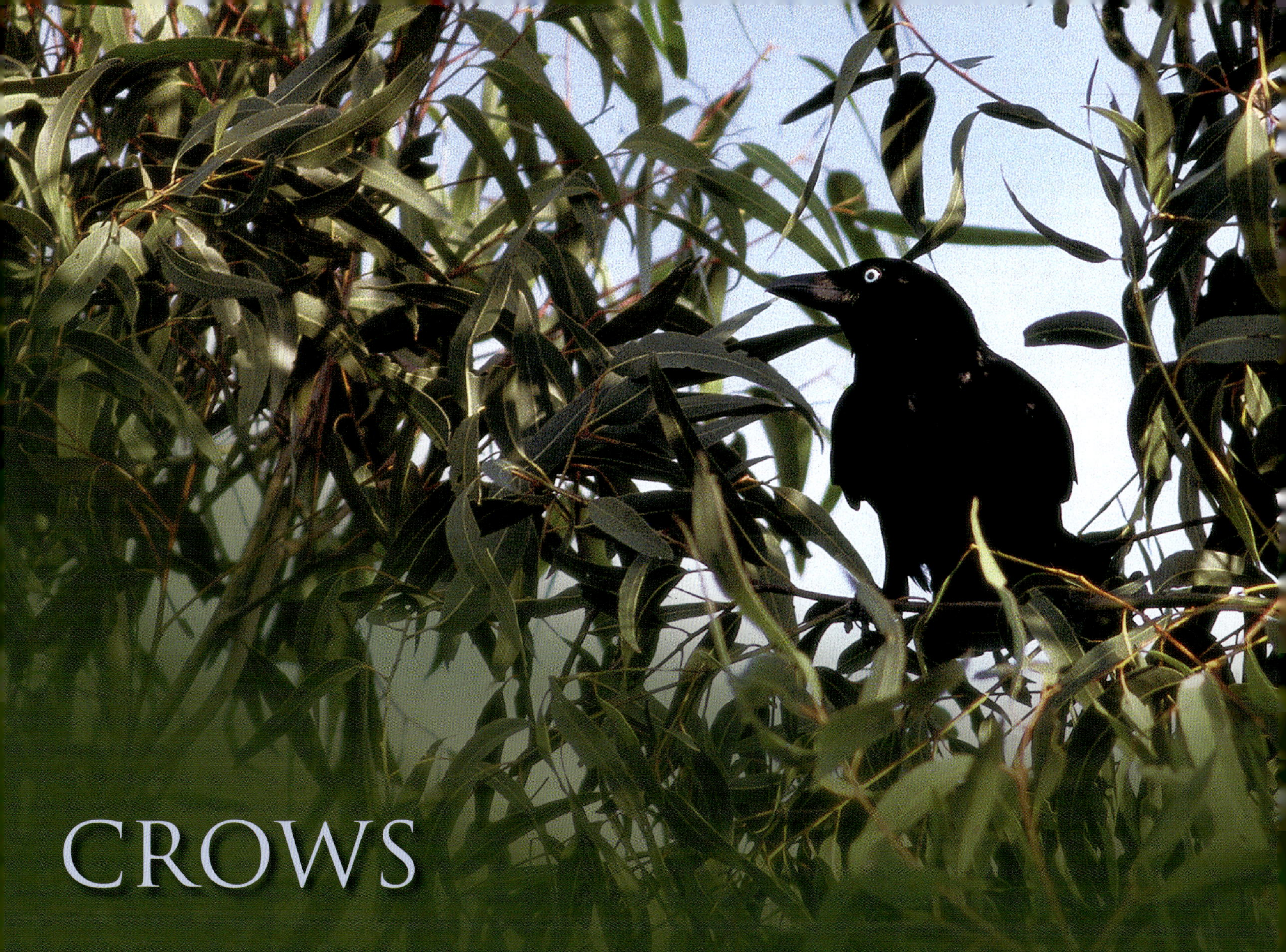

CROWS

Mother Nature, Mother Green
Has made them all to fit the scene.

Some are fed and some are eaten,
Some will win and some be beaten.

Everything goes round and round,
While we toss garbage on the ground.

And who'll take care of all the mess?
A bird, we heard, by far is best!

And, so it goes, the humble crows
Are Mother Green's Hygiene Machines.

About the Verse: Unfortunately, crows and ravens are not generally held in high regard by people. That is a pity, because crows have an important environmental role, and they are beautiful, clever, and loyally devoted to their families.

Crows are scavengers and the most valuable service they provide to humankind is cleaning up after them. If they disappeared tomorrow, we would soon notice their absence. Perhaps if they had a more attractive song, they might cause less irritation.

PLATYPUS

Platypus, platypus, you're strange, I have heard,
The fur of a mouse and the beak of a bird.
You've feet like a frog and no ears in sight –
They say that you only come out in the night!

Platypus, platypus, where are you now?
I would like to see you but I don't know how!
You won't see me out when the days are so hot,
I'm in my cool burrow, I'm curled in a knot.

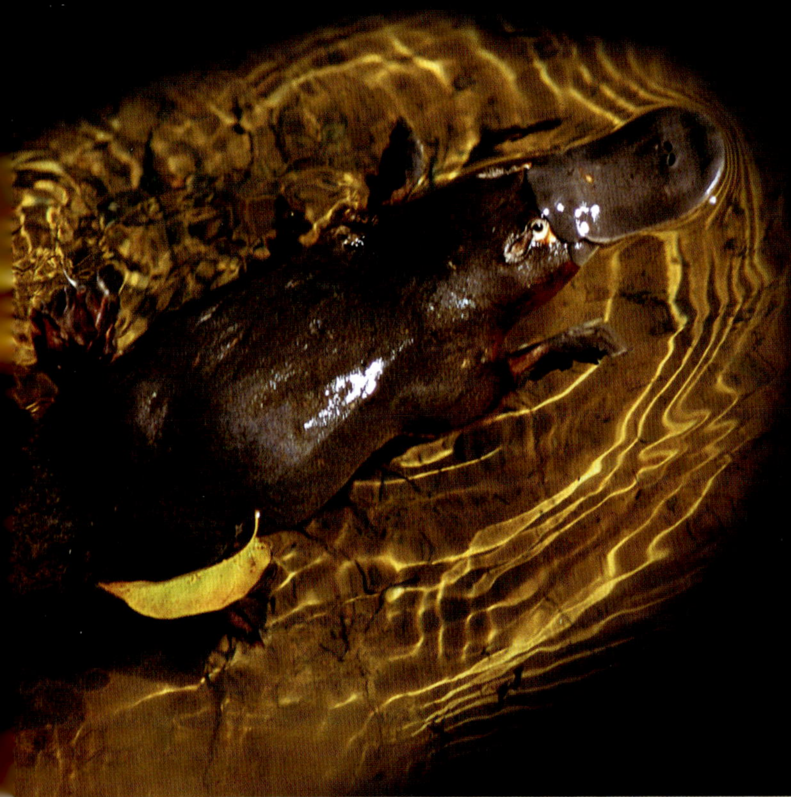

Platypus, platypus where can you be?
I'm down in the creek but I'm quite hard to see.
In winter in daytime is when I'm about,
You'll have to be quiet, you really can't shout.

Platypus, platypus, I saw you go past!
Yes, that was me and you've seen me at last.
I'm just as they said, and to me I'm not strange,
I'm what Mother Nature can do for a change!

About the Verse: Platypus is derived from the Greek *platypous*, meaning "broadfooted", an apt description. It is odd that a native animal's common name should come from ancient Greek (with a Latin ending), but the history of its naming reveals all.

The scientist who first described the Platypus used the genus Platypus as there was no suitable genus to place this bizarre animal into. That description was published.

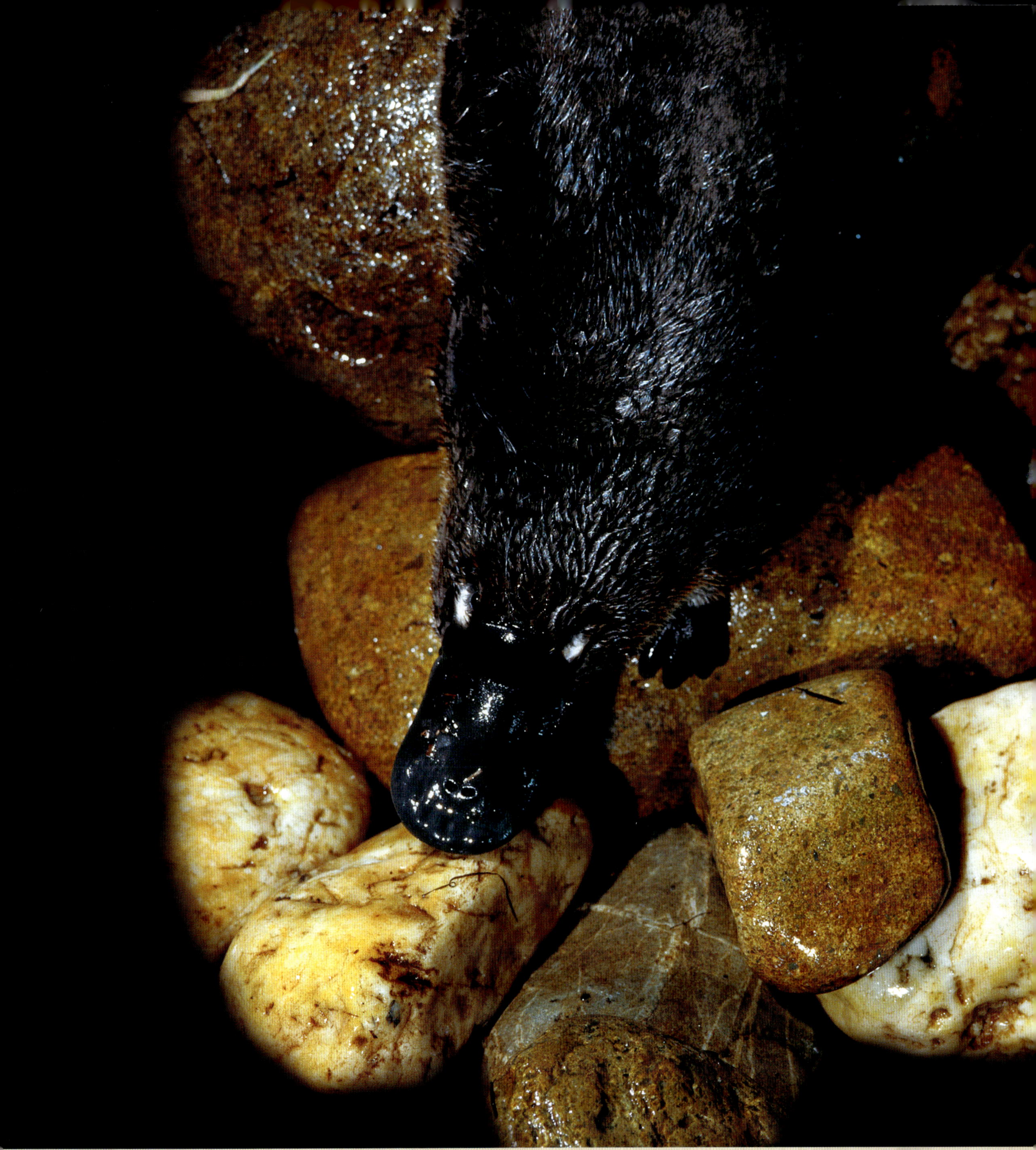

Then it was discovered that Platypus had already been used for some broad-footed beetles, known as Ambrosia Beetles, from South America. A new genus had to be thought of.

Ornithorhynchus (from two Greek words, *ornis*=bird and *rhynchos*=snout) was chosen because of the Platypus's duck-like bill, and became the new genus. But the original generic name stuck as a common name.

TINY BATS

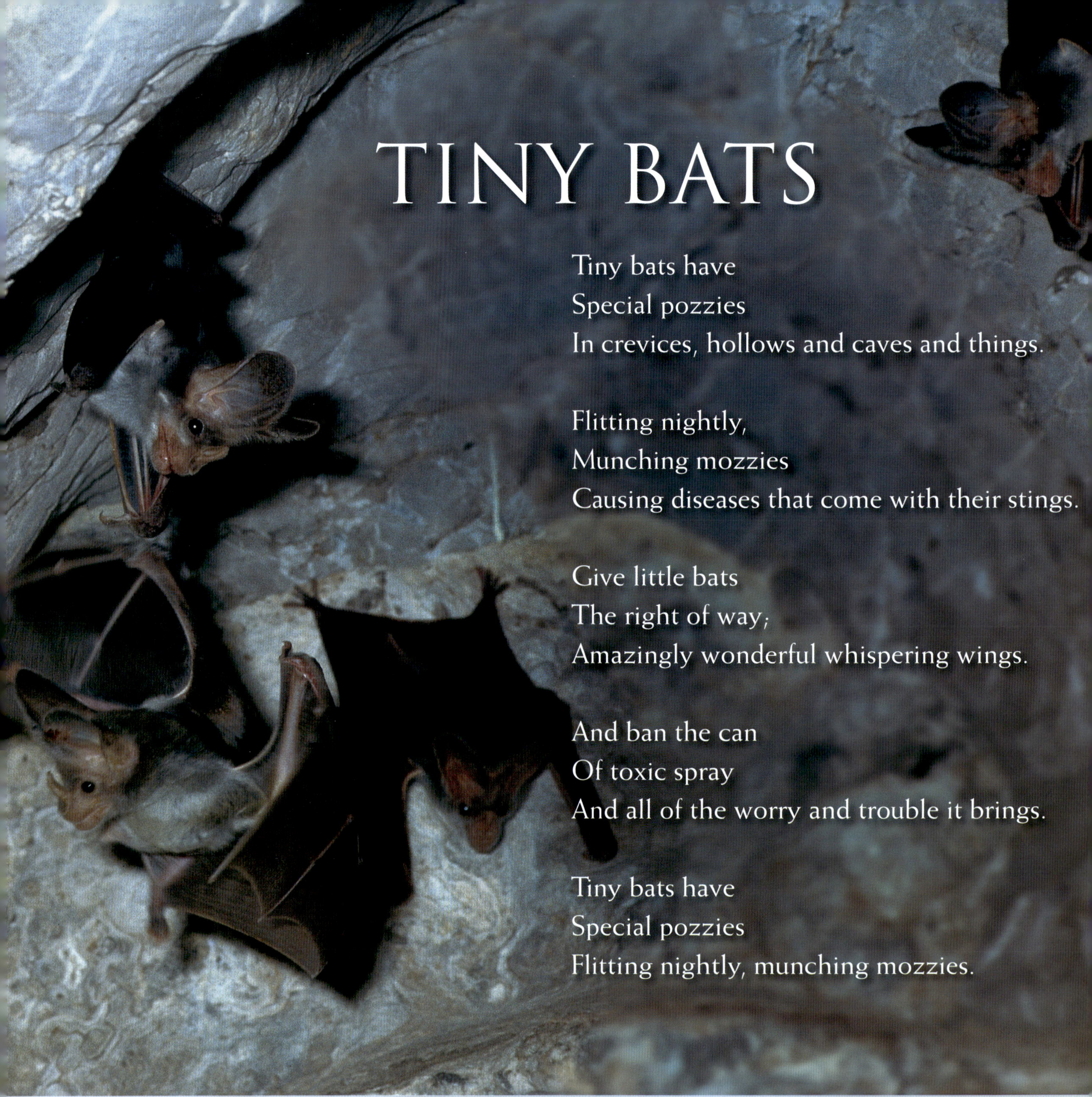

Tiny bats have
Special pozzies
In crevices, hollows and caves and things.

Flitting nightly,
Munching mozzies
Causing diseases that come with their stings.

Give little bats
The right of way;
Amazingly wonderful whispering wings.

And ban the can
Of toxic spray
And all of the worry and trouble it brings.

Tiny bats have
Special pozzies
Flitting nightly, munching mozzies.

About the Verse: Although shrouded in myth and mystery, insectivorous bats, or microbats, are beneficial to humans. They eat insects, many of which can be harmful to humans.

Although no bats are actually blind, microbats all use echolocation or "sonar" to assist in both navigation and location of prey.

In this complex process, high frequency pulses produced in the larynx are fired out of the mouth or nostrils. The sounds which rebound from stationary and moving objects are then analysed in a special section of the brain giving the bats a coarse-grained "picture" of their surrounds. It is a marvel of evolution.

BOOBOOK

A winter's night
In bright moonlight
And tiny leaves are falling.

The trees so dark,
Across the park
A Boobook Owl is calling.

On silent wings
The Boobook swings
Beneath the branches' awning.

"Hoo hoo," so deep,
Go back to sleep,
The Boobook Owl was calling.

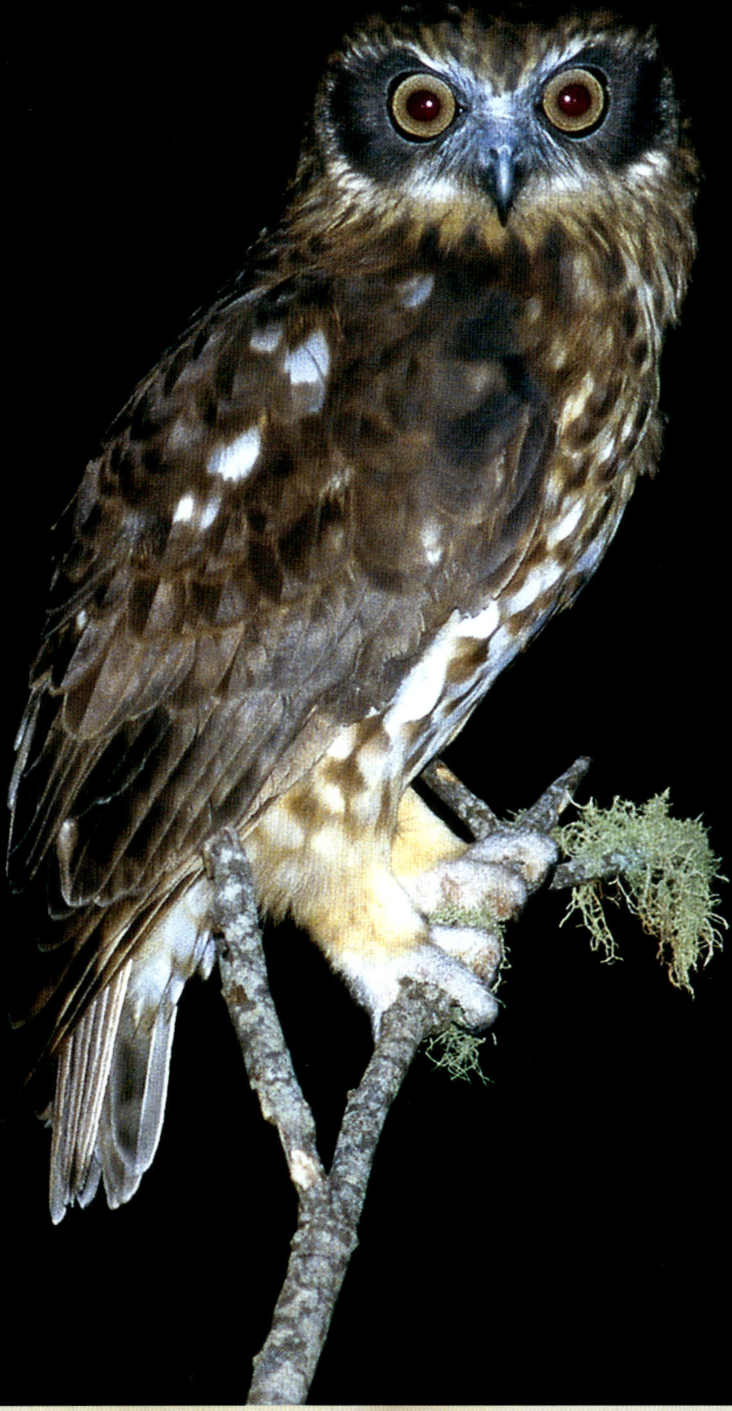

About the Verse: The smallest but best known of Australia's hawk-owls is the Boobook. Its soothing two-note "boo-book" call is well known to most people and can be heard at night throughout the land, especially in the cooler months leading to spring. Its voice is even heard in many of the inner suburbs of the large capital cities. Other names such as Mopoke and Morepork are similarly onomatopoeic words imitating its territorial call. Boobook is believed to have been one of the indigenous names for the bird.

RINGTAIL POSSUM

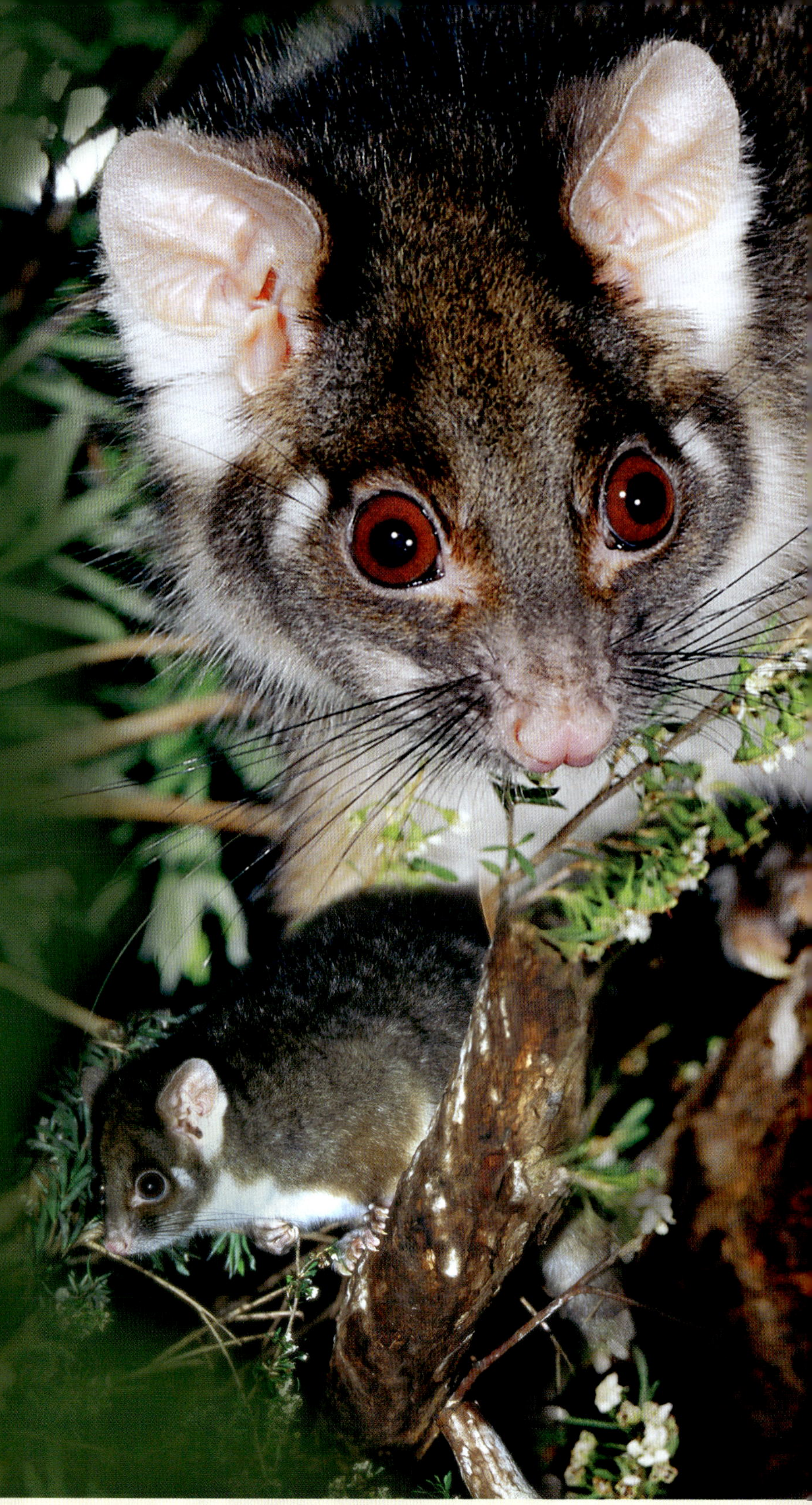

In pitchest black and darkest night
The Ringtail Possum creeps;
With bulging eyes and careful tread
Her favourite food she seeks.

Twin babies now upon her back
That once were in her pouch;
She senses danger from an owl
And freezes in a crouch.

The peril's gone and she moves on
To feed amongst the flowers;
The babies bravely forage out
Above, the huge tree towers.

Through velvet skies a hint of light
She calls them to the drey;
The dawn is drawing closer now
And soon it will be day.

About the Verse: There are six species of Ringtail Possums with at least one in every Australian State.

Most possums and gliders shelter in naturally occurring hollows, but a Ringtail constructs a drey (or dray), a shelter of twigs, leaves, shredded bark and vines. The word drey describes northern-hemisphere squirrels' shelters and was adopted in Australia.

The drey is used as a daytime shelter and is large enough to accommodate a female and up to three joeys.

The Common Ringtail Possum has not only survived the massive changes caused by European occupation, but has actually managed to thrive even in the suburbs.

Wildlife Facts

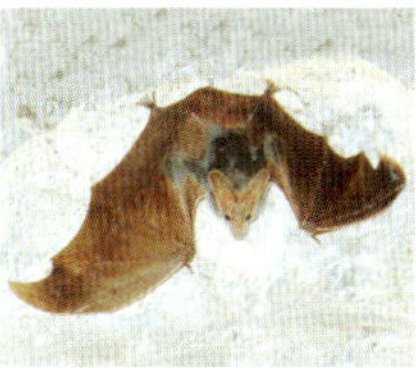

BAT, TINY (page 20)
Bats are the only mammals that can fly. A bat's wings are made of thin skin, or membrane. Some tiny bats live in caves. At night, as they fly they use echolocation to find food and to navigate. Sounds they produce bounce off objects back to the bats.

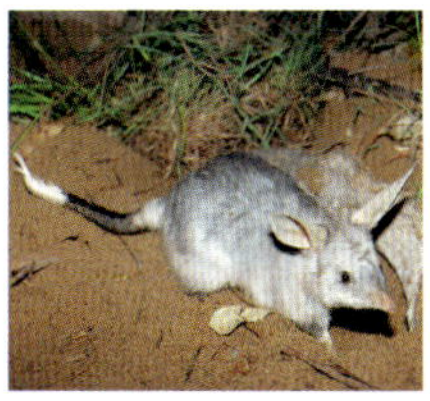

BILBY (page 12)
A Bilby is a rare kind of bandicoot that has long ears. Bilbies live in the desert. During the day, they stay cool in their burrow. Bilbies come out to find food at night. They eat insects, seeds, bulbs and fungi. Like many Australian mammals, Bilbies are marsupials and the female carries her babies in a pouch.

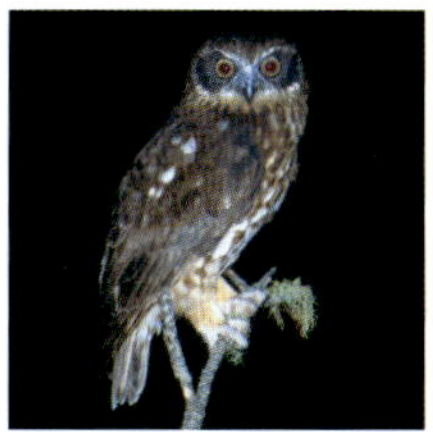

BOOBOOK (page 21)
The Southern Boobook is a small, dark-coloured owl. Boobooks are named for the sound they make, and their feathers form circular shapes around their eyes. They live all over Australia, even in city suburbs. At night they hunt for small animals to eat.

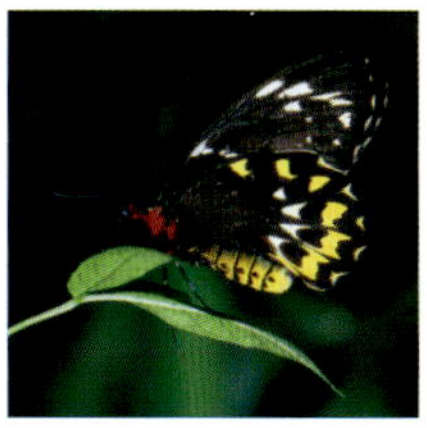

BUTTERFLY, RICHMOND BIRDWING (page 11)
The Richmond Birdwing Butterfly was once common on the central east coast of Australia. For the butterfly to survive, it must lay its eggs only on native Pararistolochia vines, which grow in rainforests along the east coast of Australia. Now that only 1% of those rainforests survive, the vines are rare. A further threat is an introduced vine that attracts females to lay their eggs: it is toxic to the newly hatched caterpillars.

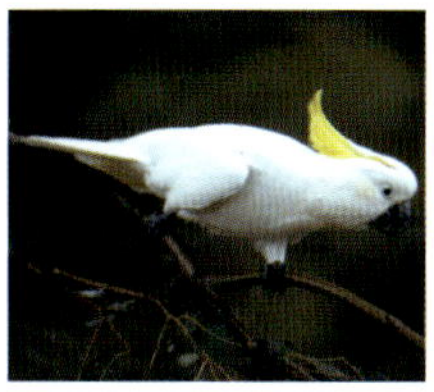

COCKATOO (pages 2 and 3)
Sulphur-crested Cockatoos are white parrots with yellow crests. A cockatoo fans its crest when it gets excited. Cockatoos are sometimes kept as pets, and they mimic even human and machine sounds. In the wild, they live in large flocks.

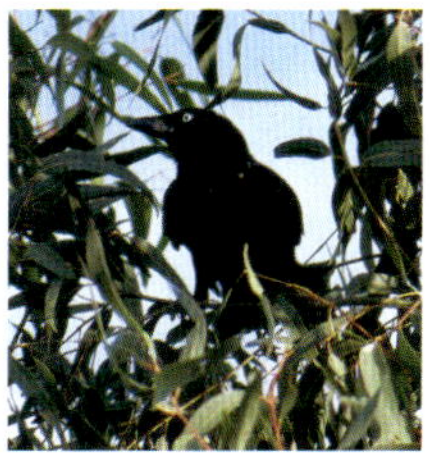

CROW (page 17)
Crows are found almost everywhere in Australia. Crows belong to the same species as ravens, and there is little difference between them. There are three native Australian ravens and two crows. They were named after the black birds in Britain that look the same. Only very close observation reveals the differences.

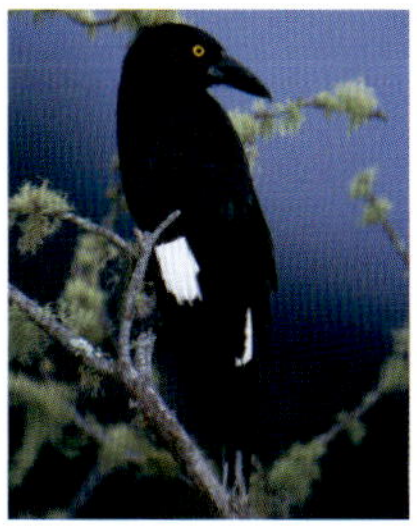

CURRAWONG (page 13)
Currawongs are black and white or grey birds with yellow eyes. There are three species – the one in the photographs is a Pied Currawong. They are named after the sound of their loud, ringing calls. Currawongs eat small lizards, insects and berries. They sometimes hang their prey in a tree fork or on a hook.

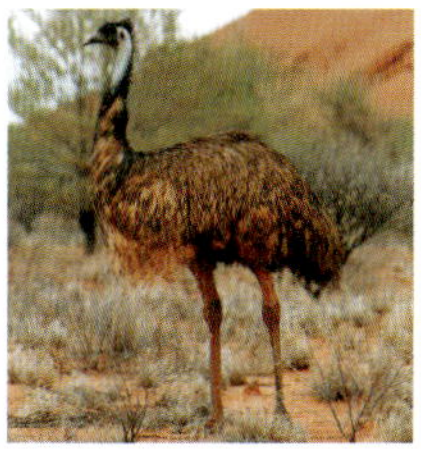

EMU (page 10)
The Emu is Australia's largest bird. There used to be three different kinds of Emu, but two are extinct. Emus can run very fast, but they cannot fly. They may grow as tall as adult humans. Female Emus lay large green eggs. After the female lays the eggs, the male incubates them and protects the chicks when they hatch.

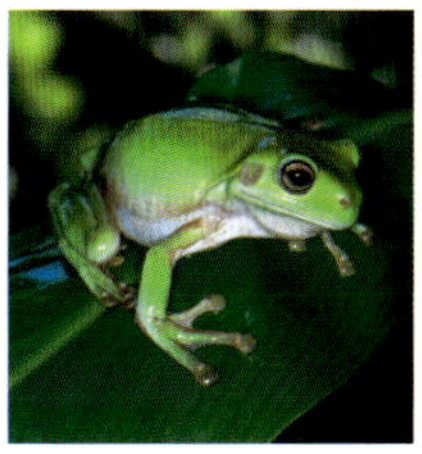

FROG (page 5)
A frog is an animal with soft, moist skin. Many frogs have large hind legs that propel them forward in a hopping motion. There are many different kinds of frogs. Some live in the ground; others live in trees or in cracks in rocks. Most frogs need clean water or a damp place to lay their eggs in. Tiny tadpoles that breathe through gills hatch from the eggs. As the tadpoles grow they lose their tails and grow legs. Adult frogs breathe air.

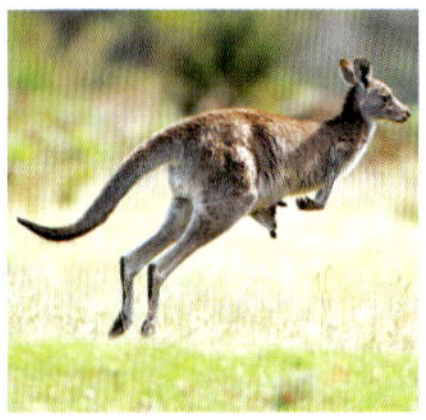

KANGAROO (page 7)

Kangaroos live in groups called "mobs". They spend the day resting in shady places, then graze on grass and leaves in the morning and late afternoon. A baby kangaroo is called a joey. It lives in its mother's pouch until it is big enough to hop around and find its own food. There are lots of different kinds of kangaroos in Australia. Small kangaroos are called wallabies. The most common kangaroos are the Eastern Grey Kangaroo and the Red Kangaroo.

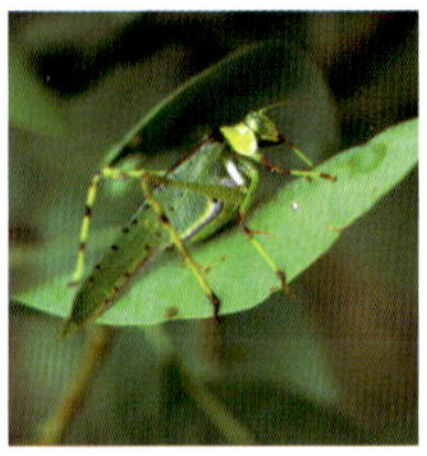

KATYDID (page 16)

Katydids are insects similar to crickets. They have long feelers. Katydids have strong back legs like grasshoppers: they are also called Long-horned Grasshoppers. Katydids call from amongst leaves, but crickets call from the ground.

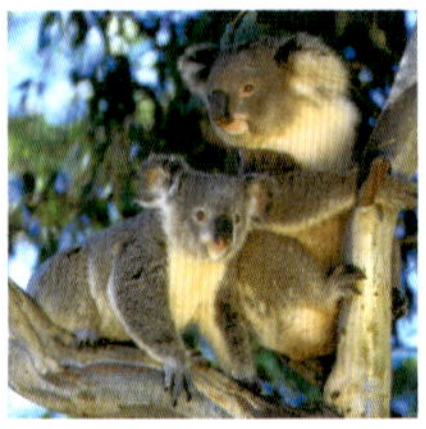

KOALA (page 4)

Koalas live high in the branches of gum trees. They spend most of their time sleeping. For a few hours each day they eat gum leaves, and this diet generates little energy. A baby Koala is called a joey and lives in its mother's pouch for about six months then rides on her back for about another six months.

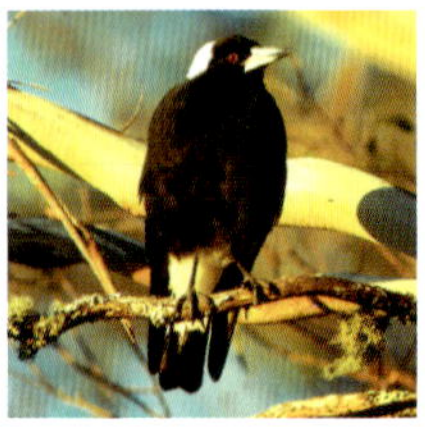

MAGPIE (page 6)

There is only one species of Australian Magpie, and they are found throughout Australia. Their plumage may vary from place to place and they go by different common names. They often feed and nest near people's houses. Magpies have strong melodious calls that they use to keep in touch with family members or to warn other groups that an area is theirs.

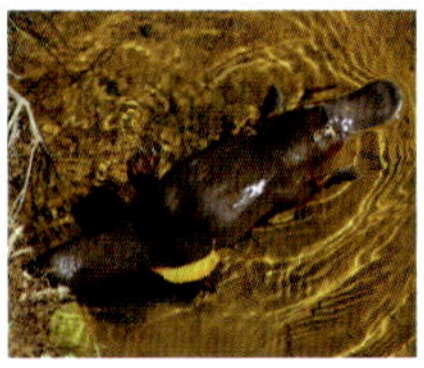

PLATYPUS (pages 18 and 19)

The Platypus has thick waterproof fur that keeps it warm in cool water. Its bill is rubbery and has sensors that detect tiny electric signals given out by small aquatic animals such as worms. Its prey is stored in cheek pouches then eaten at the surface.

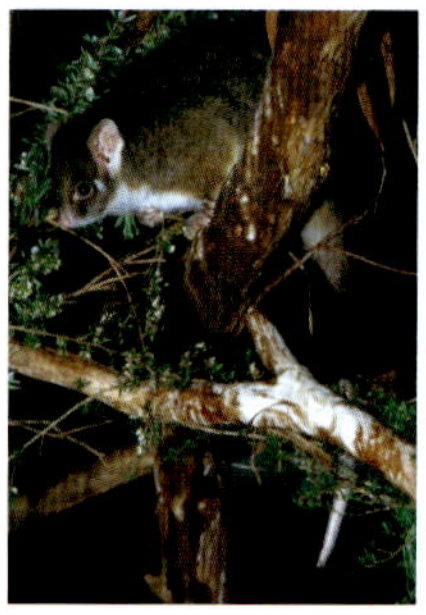

POSSUM, RINGTAIL (page 22)

Ringtail Possums are named for their curling tails, which may also act as a "fifth limb" carrying the weight of the possum's whole body, if necessary. Possums come out at night to feed on leaves, flowers and fruit. Some possums eat insects. A baby possum starts growing in its mother's pouch. At about four months old, it will ride on her back.

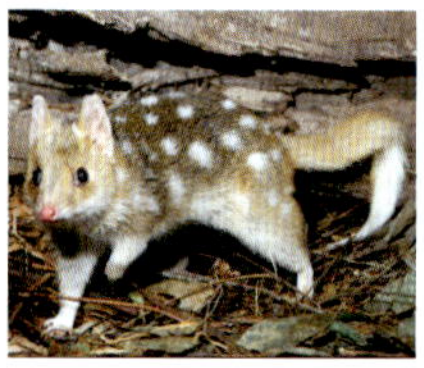

QUOLL (page 9)

Quolls are cat-sized, spotted marsupials that live in forests. They are still often called "native cats". Quolls hunt smaller animals for food. Quolls have disappeared from many areas of Australia as the forests they live in are cleared. The Northern Quoll population has declined since the arrival of the poisonous Cane Toad. Quolls compete with cats and foxes for food, and are sometimes eaten by their competitors.

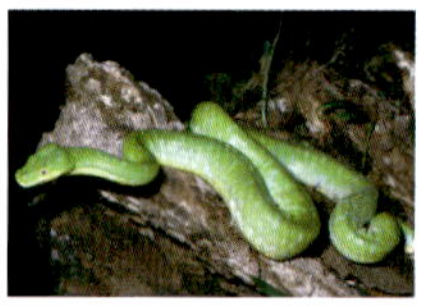

SNAKE (page 8)

Snakes are long, slender reptiles that have no legs. They are cold-blooded, so they have to use heat from the sun to warm themselves. Some snakes bite with their fangs, others wrap around their prey in a coil. Snakes swallow the animals they eat whole. Most snakes will avoid humans if they can, and will bite only if they think the person is a threat.

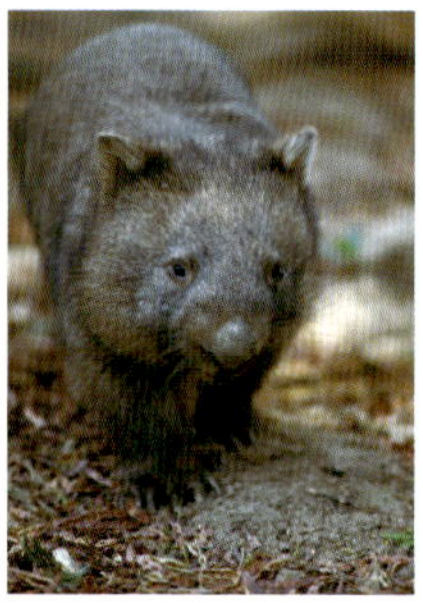

WOMBAT (pages 14 and 15)

Wombats are marsupials. A tiny newborn grows in its mother's pouch. The female wombat's pouch faces backwards with the result that, when she digs a burrow, the dirt does not get inside the pouch. The burrow is a place for sleeping and hiding from enemies. Wombats have strong front legs and claws for digging. They feed, mainly at night, on grass and leaves.